THE SCIENCE OF

ANIME

MECHA-NOIDS AND AI-SUPER-BOTS

LOIS H. GRESH AND
ROBERT WEINBERG

THUNDER'S MOUTH PRESS
NEW YORK

THE SCIENCE OF ANIME
Mecha-Noids and AI-Super-Bots

Published by
Thunder's Mouth Press
An Imprint of Avalon Publishing Group Inc.
245 West 17th Street, 11th Floor
New York, NY 10011

AVALON
publishing group incorporated

First printing December 2005

Library of Congress Cataloging-in-Publication Data is available.

ISBN: 1-56025-768-7
ISBN: 13: 978-1-56025-768-4

9 8 76 5 4 3 2 1

Book design by Maria Elias
Printed in the United States of America
Distributed by Publishers Group West

To Bob Weinberg, for everything
                    Lois Gresh

To Brad, Natalie, and Brady; to Brian
and Beth; and to the original Astro-Boy
for getting me started
                    Bob Weinberg

Contents

Introduction

Welcome to *The Science of Anime*. As with any good science book, we think it's only proper to start with a few definitions.

Anime: According to the dictionary, anime is a style of animation that developed in Japan characterized by stylized colorful art and futuristic settings, and usually filled with sex and violence. Once upon a time, some years back in the late 1970s, anime was better known in the United States as Japanimation, but that term was deemed racist and derogatory, and the term *anime* was used in its stead. Despite the dictionary definition, however, not all anime deals with the future. There is plenty of historical anime, adventure anime, romance anime, and even anime dealing with high school tennis matches. Anime simply means animation from Japan, and that's about the only truly defining characteristic.

Science: Science is a branch of study concerned with observing and classifying facts and attempting to discover general laws about those facts. The technique used to discover these laws is called the scientific method. The four steps of the scientific method are: observing data; formulating a hypothesis about them; testing the hypothesis to see if it holds true for the specific case; then testing it for the general case. If the experiments show the hypothesis to be true, sooner or later it becomes known as a theory or a law. There's a general misunderstanding about science, in that many nonscientists think that a theory is just a guess, and not based on facts. In fact, a theory is a concept that has been rigorously tested again and again and shown to be true in all circumstances. Physics, biology, chemistry, and other sciences all rely on laws and theories.

The Science of Anime: This book is our attempt to take a look at various anime series, ranging from TV classics like *Mobile Suit Gundam* and *Neon Genesis Evangelion* to spectacular feature-length animated movies like *Akira* and *Ghost in the Shell,* and explore the scientific facts and fiction used in these works. While many anime series were made up entirely from the imagination of the writer, a good number were based on the latest scientific facts and theories of the time. In this book, we'll take a look at the most interesting scientific ideas used in anime and investigate whether they're actually on the cutting edge of science or whether they lurk only in the depths of our imaginations.

Please note that we chose this title for a reason. While we both enjoy non–science fiction (SF) anime—Lois is a fan of *Dragonball Z*, and Bob enjoys the exploits of the *Prince of Tennis*—such shows will not be discussed in this book. We investigate only those anime shows that feature interesting science and technology concepts.

Sometimes those concepts will be vague or unrealistic; in other shows they will be on the cutting edge of today's scientific discoveries. That's what we aim to find out—in addition to taking you on an entertaining and informative journey.

And, as a brief side note that we always like to include in our books, *The Science of Anime* is a collaboration between two writers and friends, Lois H. Gresh and Robert Weinberg. The entire book was written back and forth over the Internet, and while we each composed about half of the first draft of the book, we revised and revised each other's work so that no one page can be labeled entirely Lois or entirely Bob. This book is a mixture of our thoughts, tastes, and opinions. So when we use the word "we" in discussing some topic in the text, we're not being snobbish or pretending to be royalty. We really mean "We, the two of us."

Now on to what we discovered about anime!

1. The Origins of Anime

The Birth of Comics and Anime

To fully understand the science of anime, we must first understand both its origins and its place in modern Japanese society. To do that, we need to take a close look at *manga*, the Japanese printed art form on which almost all anime is based. We also need to study the origins of comic books in the United States as well as the beginnings of animated film there, since both genres play an important role in the development of modern manga and anime. In fact, though the roots of comic book literature are quite different in the two countries, in many ways, they are also very similar.

In Japan, the earliest examples of illustrated stories were picture scrolls created by Buddhist monks as far back as the sixth and seventh centuries. These scrolls ran the length of the parchment, telling a story and using common symbols such as cherry blossoms and red leaves to indicate the passage of time. The most famous such scroll was drawn by Bishop Toba in the twelfth century and was named the "Choujuugiga," or "the animal scroll." The story showed animals behaving like humans and satirized Buddhist priests.

In the thirteenth century, common people began drawing images of the afterlife on the walls of temples. The artwork was crude and exaggerated, but in many ways resembled the art of modern Japan. Over the centuries, these drawings on temple walls remained popular, though the topics they illustrated varied and were not all religious in nature.

By the seventeenth century, such pictures had become so famous that they began appearing as separate illustrations on wood blocks. These blocks with pictures on them were known as *Edo,* and their subjects were most often erotic. The pictures were done in monochrome, with basic outlines, no shading and using blocks of color to highlight certain parts of the illustration.

In 1702, Shumboko Ono, a famous Edo artist, assembled an entire book of Edo prints and labeled them with captions. This first book of wood-block prints was more a collection of individual pictures than a true narrative. Still, it set the stage for similar books combining stories and ink-brush illustrations that appeared over the next hundred years. The book form allowed the story to come alive and the illustrations to be more narrative. This style of heavily illustrated narrative was known as Toba-e, and such volumes soon became the most popular form of Japanese literature. The name Toba-e was a tribute to Bishop Toba (1053-1140), the creator of the "animal scroll."

The publication of Toba-e books marked the start of the commercialization of book publishing in Japan at the beginning of the eighteenth century. Toba-e books spread from Osaka to Kyoto, Nagoya, and then to Edo (today's Tokyo) during the Tokugawa period.

In 1815, the term manga was invented by the artist Katsushika Hokusai. Hokusai lived from 1760 to 1849 and created over thirty thousand illustrations. His most famous picture was the wood-block "The Great Wave," which became closely identified with traditional Japanese art. The illustration showed a huge ocean wave overwhelming Mount Fuji. Hokusai's term for his Toba-e art was derived from the words *man,* meaning "oneself" or "whimsical," and the word *ga,* meaning "picture." Thus, manga means "picture of oneself" or "whimsical picture." Others have translated manga to mean "involuntary sketches" or "unintentional pictures." All definitions seem to work. Manga was soon adopted as the name for these popular illustrated books.

In the nineteenth century, the most popular mangas were called *ukiyo-e*, or "pictures of the floating world." These pictures were often erotic, and primarily depicted the pleasures of theaters, restaurants, teahouses, geishas, and courtesans of Tokyo. Many prints were in fact posters, advertising theater performances and brothels, or portraits of popular actors and beautiful teahouse girls. Actual storytelling was still not a part of most manga.

Meanwhile, in the United States, illustration was following a different path. Benjamin Franklin published the first cartoon in a newspaper in the United States in 1754. It was a picture of a severed snake cut into pieces, representing the thirteen colonies, with the words "Join or Die" printed beneath the picture. Artwork had been published in books and newspapers before this, but Franklin's cartoon was the first melding of a picture and words to make a point without referring to any other text. The concept of political cartoons proved popular, and editorial cartoons flourished in the United States for the next hundred years. It wasn't until 1896, however, that an artist came up with the idea of using a cartoon to tell a joke, and not merely to make a political point.

The first newspaper comic panel done in a single-box format was Richard Fenton Outcalt's creation *The Yellow Kid*. It ran as a weekly feature in Joseph Pulitzer's newspaper the *World*. The strip started as a black-and-white one-panel gag cartoon, but the newspaper engravers were experimenting with color and added yellow to the Kid's outfit, thus transforming him into "*The Yellow Kid.*"

The Yellow Kid proved to be a huge success, and in the newspaper business at the time, success immediately bred competition. Soon after *The Yellow Kid* appeared in the *World*, William Randolph Hearst began running a similar humorous comic strip, *Little Bears*, by James Swinnerton, in *his* newspaper, the *Journal American*. Both strips were immensely popular, but they still were only one-panel cartoon illustrations. And neither could match the popularity of the next comic feature, Rudolph Dirk's *Katzenjammer Kids*, which first appeared on December 12, 1897, in the *Journal American*.

The Katzenjammer Kids was a revolutionary comic strip. Instead of consisting of only one panel, as was the case with other comics up to that time, it contained several panels that progressed in logical order, thus telling a story. Dialogue, which had before been kept strictly at the bottom of the strip, was inserted into the panels inside word balloons that indicated the speaker. Plus, since four-color presses had by this time moved into the newspaper field, the strips were printed in color.

The Katzenjammer Kids proved so popular that it started a comic-strip war between the various newspaper chains of the period. Hearst and Pulitzer fought over every new comic strip artist and writer, trying to make sure the best of the bunch worked for their papers, and only their papers. Not that there was any real problem finding material. By the first decade of the twentieth century, there were over 150 different newspaper strips being published in national newspapers. The two things these many strips had in common was that they were all humorous in nature, and they all had little or no continuity. Comic strips were meant to be read the day they were published and then forgotten. All such cartoons were labeled "comics" because they were funny. As a group they were known as "comic strips." Comic strips flourished not only in the United States, but in Europe and Asia as well.

When Japan was opened to the outside world by Commodore Perry in 1854, the event brought great economic and social changes to the country. New printing techniques were introduced that were much more efficient than wood-block prints. These methods made publishing commercially financially viable. In the years that followed Perry's visit, the paintings of European artists introduced shading, perspective, and anatomy to Japanese illustrators. Influenced by European tastes, the Japanese began publishing humor magazines resembling the British magazine, *Punch,* the most famous of which was *Marumaru Chimbun,* which began in 1877.

American comic strips were a huge hit in turn-of-the-century Japan. Moreover, the style and structure of the comics themselves had a profound influence on Japanese artists. Comic strips, with their word balloons and the notion of separate panels for action taking place over time, revolutionized storytelling in Japan. Only a short time after the introduction of comics to Japan, well-known manga artists like Rakuten Kitazawa and Ippei Okamoto were drawing their own newspaper strips. As in the United States, these early newspaper comics led to paperbound collections of strips, called *comics* in the United States, *manga* in Japan.

Several major changes took place in the United States in the 1920s in the comic strip field. The first was the realization that not all comics had to be funny. The second was the idea that, since customers regularly read their favorite comics every day of the week, continuity in comics was not necessarily evil. These two revolutionary ideas led to the beginning of nonhumorous daily strips. *Wash Tubbs,* created by Roy Crane in 1924, was the first adventure comic strip. Action and story continued from day to day and, over a long period of time, the comic strip told a complete story. *Wash Tubbs* was a huge hit, and it was immediately followed by a number of other story strips. Even humor strips began to feature continuity and story lines in their gags.

In 1929, science fiction was introduced to the comic strip with a trio of new adventure strips: *Buck Rogers, Tarzan,* and *Flash Gordon.* All three strips were incredibly popular. Science fiction, still relatively new as a literary genre when compared with mysteries or westerns, was the fastest-selling concept in newspaper comics.

Hoping to make some extra money from these popular strips, several newspaper syndicates (companies that owned and distributed the strips to papers across the country) decided in the 1930s to publish reprint collections of comics in cheap paperbound books. The idea was to provide monthly compilations of strips so that readers who had missed some episodes could catch up on what they missed. Also, new readers could be hooked by making an entire story line—that had played out over the course of a month in the newspaper—available in one purchase. These early comic strip collections, usually featuring a color cover of one of the characters, became known as comic books.

The first such reprint comic, titled *Famous Funnies* and published by Eastern Color Co., was dated July 1934. While it took a few months to generate a profit, *Famous Funnies* was soon an established hit. In the United States of the time, nothing bred competition like success. Several other reprint books were launched in short order, and the comic book field was born.

While American comic strips easily made the transition from newspaper to book form, they did not have as much luck with the movies. Animation was Hollywood's answer to comic strips. Black-and-white cartoon characters had silly adventures on screen in a gray world. Comic book characters couldn't compete with real-life clowns like the Marx Brothers or Charlie Chaplin, and they remained an entertaining but minor novelty in theaters. Of the several comic book characters whose creators tried to make the move from newspaper to screen, only Popeye met with much success.

Back in Japan, manga artists were among the leaders of illustrators working in the new field of animation. The first successful Japanese animated film was Seitaro Kitayama's *Momotaro*, released in 1918. Unfortunately, it was around this time that the military element of the Japanese government came to realize that animation and manga could be used for more than entertainment —they were excellent vehicles for propaganda.

Manga books remained humorous, but now the humor was based partly on satire and partly on propaganda. Artists were told what to draw, and more important, what not to draw. Those artists who cooperated with the government were treated well, while those who refused were imprisoned and forbidden to write. Artists who had spent much of their careers drawing humor strips critical of the government suddenly found themselves writing material totally at odds with their earlier work. During the war years, cartoonists were allowed to draw three types of comic strips: single-panel jokes about Japan's enemies; family comic strips that portrayed home life during a war; and propaganda. Cartoons served pretty much the same purpose. The years before and during World War II were a low point in Japanese manga and animation.

In the United States, meanwhile, comics and cartoons took off in unexpected directions. At first, newspaper comic strips had been aimed at adults. Early cartoons from the Disney and Fleischer studios were aimed at both adults and children. The humor of such material was universal, and there was no sense that comics or cartoons were just for kids. But then, in 1938, the comic book world changed forever.

Comic books up to that time had been exclusively reprint volumes, filled with copies of daily strips that had run in the newspapers months earlier. The problem with such books was that only a few strips were popular enough that a comic book could be sold for a dime. There were only so many *Buck Rogers* and *Tarzan* strips to promote a comic book. Plus, the newspaper publishers and the syndicates, like King Features and Universal Press Syndicate, who controlled the rights to the most popular strips wanted high fees for the reprint rights to their comics. The comic book field was profitable—but only for the few.

The man who saw a way around these difficulties was pulp fiction writer Major Malcolm Wheeler-Nicholson. He reasoned that if reprint material sold in comic books, so would new stories. Equally appealing to Wheeler-Nicholson was the fact that in publishing new and unknown material, he wouldn't have to pay its creators nearly as much as he did for reprints. He hired mostly unknown writers and artists to create entirely new comic book stories and published them in a comic book he called *More Fun Comics*.

The first issue of *More Fun* appeared in February 1935, but the comic never achieved the success Wheeler-Nicholson wanted. The comic book stories he published just weren't as good as the ones being reprinted from newspapers, and readers wanted only the best. Wheeler-Nicholson had discovered a way to publish inexpensive comic books, but he sacrificed quality for profit and ended up with neither. After a short time, he took on two partners, Harry Donenfeld and Jack Liebowitz. Their money kept *More Fun* going despite lackluster sales. Wheeler-Nicholson added two more titles to his line, *New Adventure* and *Detective Comics*, but by 1938 he was broke.

Wheeler-Nicholson sold his interest in the publishing company to his two partners. Still hoping for a winning comic, Donenfeld and Liebowitz decided to try one more title: *Action Stories*. Featured as the lead character in the first issue of the new comic book, dated June 1938, was a character called "Superman," created originally as a comic strip character but never sold to the newspapers. The superhero from Krypton turned out to be a huge hit, and within a few short months, the age of comic book superheroes was born.

Superman did more than save original comic books. He changed the way comic books were perceived by the American public, forever. Because newspaper comics were aimed at adults, so were comics like *New Funnies,* which reprinted newspaper comics. Even Buck Rogers—science fiction or not—was aimed at a teenage to young-adult audience. But not so Superman. He was too simple, too primitive, too much wish-fulfillment to be a believable character. Comic book creations like Superman—and

Batman, who followed soon afterward—and Green Arrow, Hawkman, Wonder Woman, and the Human Torch, and many others, the public felt, were aimed at kids.

Specifically, these new characters appeared to have been created for children ranging in age from eight to eighteen. Comic books, originally published for adults, were from henceforth judged by the American public to be reading material for the nation's children. And that was that.

This perception spread slowly but surely across the face of America to Hollywood and the animation industry. Cartoons, which had always relied on sight gags for much of their humor, were suddenly seen as kids' stuff and nothing more.

Animation in the United States had never been seen as anything more than entertainment for children. Though comic strips were always recognized as entertainment for adults as well as youngsters, the same was not true for animation. In the 1930s, not all cartoons were aimed specifically at kids. The Betty Boop cartoons, for example, featuring Cab Calloway singing "Minnie the Moocher" and "St. James Infirmary," included bizarre images for children, too—but the songs were aimed at adults. Unfortunately, such cartoons were few and far between.

Disney Studios was the giant in the animation field in the 1930s and 1940s, and their cartoons were aimed strictly at children. While the antics of Donald Duck, Goofy, and Mickey Mouse had some appeal to adults, the main thrust of Disney cartoons was always toward the younger viewer. Just as most comic book companies made the marketing decision to aim their products at kids, so Disney Studios made the decision to produce their cartoons for the same audience. Comics and animated films were also used as vehicles for propaganda by the Allies, but they were not as pervasive or as heavy-handed as those produced by the Axis powers.

When World War II came to an end, comic strip and comic book art in the United States and Japan went in opposite directions. In the United States, comic books were considered kids' stuff, lacking in sophistication and style. Animated cartoons, though they did possess slightly more style and thus sometimes appealed to an older crowd, were still considered children's material. Even the feature-length cartoon movies produced by Disney through the rest of the 1940s and 1950s were viewed primarily as children's entertainment, with only a small crossover to adult markets.

In Japan, the war years and the strict censorship after the war nearly destroyed Japan's network of cartoonists and animators. The only thing the Japanese market had going for it was that manga books were not considered inferior reading material. There were manga comics for all tastes, ranging from adventure to mystery to sports to love.

The art was crudely drawn, but it told a story. Ordinary men and women read manga and followed the stories in the comics with fanlike intensity. The market for good manga existed in Japan. All it needed was a genius to reveal it.

The God of Anime

One man changed the face of Japanese manga forever. His name was Osamu Tezuka, and in his later years, he was known respect- fully as "the God of Manga." Tezuka made anime not only pos- sible but profitable. A relentless, hardworking man, he was responsible for dozens of best-selling manga books, with subjects ranging from pirate adventures to fantasy stories; there were comics aimed at boys, comics aimed at girls, and comics aimed at adults. His output was prodigious and so popular that an entire generation of manga artists grew up imitating his style of art and storytelling. His influence on modern manga and anime cannot be overstated. Without "the God of Manga," modern Japanese manga and anime would probably not exist.

Dr. Osamu Tezuka was born on November 3, 1928. As a child, Tezuka entertained himself by watching eight-millimeter movie projector reels of cartoons featuring such American characters as Mickey Mouse and Donald Duck. A tremendous fan of Disney animation, he saw the movie *Bambi* eighty times and was pro- foundly influenced by the movie's style. The young Tezuka learned how to draw by sketching illustrations for his friends much in the style of Disney artwork.

Tezuka worked as an assistant in a factory while he attended Osaka University as a medical student. It was at school that he practiced and refined his drawing technique. Though he did earn his medical degree, Tezuka never practiced medicine. Instead, he

Photo taken near the Osamu Tezuka Museum in Takerzuka, Japan. The sculpture is of Hi no Tori, the Bird of Fire (the Phoenix), which appears in many of Tezuka's anime and manga. Photo by Matthew Weinberg.

became a manga artist. His first published work was the story "Machan no Nikkicho" (Machan's Diary) for the children's magazine *Mainichi Shogakusei Shinbun*. It was published in 1946, while he was still in school. Tezuka soon became known for the "large eyes" style of his drawings of people. He based his illustrations on the cartoon characters of Walt Disney and Max Fleischer and set the standard for Japanese animation for years to come.

Tezuka's first best-selling comic, *Shin Takarajima* (New Treasure Island) appeared in 1947. The story was done using cinematic techniques in which the pictures, and not just the words, tell the story. For example, the first scene of the story has a young boy arriving in a car at a dock. In most comics and manga, such a scene would be shown in one panel. Tezuka, using close-ups and fade-outs and long-distance shots, took eight pages of art to illustrate the scene. His stories were meant to be novels in cartoon form, and *Shin Takarajima* was the first major graphic novel ever produced in the comic book field. At two hundred pages, it was an epic adventure unlike anything published in manga or comics before. It sold over 400,000 copies.

The young artist fused techniques and styles used in early motion pictures to the style of art in Disney and Fleischer cartoons. Tezuka's graphic novel featured many detailed scenes as well as art techniques normally used only in films. Incorporating zooming, panning, and close-ups of characters, Tezuka created manga art that had never been seen before. It was the beginning of the postwar manga revolution.

This success was followed three years later by "Jungle Taitei," which was published in *Manga-Shone,* another manga magazine of the period. Dozens of other successes followed in all kinds of genres, including science fiction, humor, horror, and fantasy. Tezuka created manga adaptations of *King Kong* (1947), *Faust* (1949), *Pinocchio* (1952), *Around the World in 80 Days* (1953), and *Crime and Punishment* (1953). After the science fiction feature *Lost World* in 1948, in 1951 he created *Atom Taishi,* which was later renamed *Tetsuwan Atom.* Known internationally as *Astro Boy,* this comic became Tezuka's most famous work.

Tezuka not only drew a huge *amount* of manga, he also drew many different *kinds* of manga. He didn't concentrate on one field or one area of interest, but tried to write and illustrate stories that would touch new markets. Tezuka's stories were the earliest examples of genres such as *shounen* (boys' manga), *shoujo* (girls' manga) and more. He drew dramatic manga, action-filled manga, and adult-oriented manga. Some of his best-known creations included the girls' strip *Ribon no Kishi* (Ribon the Knight), the western *Lemon Kid, Ogon no Trunk* (The Golden Trunk), and the science fiction stories *Majin Garon, O'Man, Captain Ken, Big X,* and *W3*. He also created the horror manga *Vampire,* the historical strip *Dororo,* and the medical series *Black Jack,* which was his longest-running comic. His *Adolf ni Tsugu,* an epic tale about World War II and three men named Adolf, ran over 1,000 pages.

The Osamu Tezuka Museum. Photo by Matthew Weinberg.

By drawing many different kinds of stories, Tezuka laid the groundwork for the diversity that manga still enjoys today. Tezuka's influence on Japan's popular fiction was enormous. He drew children's picture books, risqué humor for men's magazines, comic-book romantic soap operas for women's magazines, and political cartoons for newspapers. He established the notion that cartooning was an acceptable form of storytelling for any age group. As noted above, this idea was in sharp contrast to the United States, where the attitude was that cartoons and comics were for kids.

Tezuka's productivity was amazing. *The Complete Manga Works of Tezuka Osamu,* a set of his best work published in Japan, comprises some 400 volumes—over 80,000 pages. In fact, it's been estimated that his total work included over 700 mangas in about 170,000 pages—and even that count is not quite comprehensive.

It is impossible to overestimate the importance of Tezuka to the culture of modern Japan. Before he began writing and illustrating for manga magazines, most children in Japan stopped reading comics when they started high school. However, Tezuka's work was so popular that children raised on his manga didn't want to give up reading him as they grew older. They demanded he continue writing stories for teenagers, and, later on, adults. Thus, during the late 1950s, manga made the jump from merely being children's literature to being stories for all ages. That's something that never happened in the United States.

By the late 1960s, Tezuka and other popular illustrators had

THE ORIGINS OF ANIME

turned manga into something far more than mere children's books. In a way, manga evolved with its audience and with the maturing tastes of its audience. As the readers of manga matured, so did the story lines in manga. Though sales of comic books ebbed and flowed in the United States, by the last decade of the twentieth century, manga accounted for over 40 percent of all the books being published in Japan.

In 1956, weekly magazines were introduced in Japan, and in 1959, a number of children's weekly magazines began publication. Originally, these kids' magazines were a mix of entertainment, education, and manga. It wasn't long before the various publishers noted that the magazines with the most manga sold the best. So, they increased the amount of manga in their magazines, and circulation soared.

Jump, a magazine that published manga aimed primarily at young boys, began publication in 1968. It was in *Jump* that Akira Toriyama's hit series, *Dragonball,* first appeared. In 1980, *Jump* was selling three million copies a month. In 1985, it sold over four million a month, and in 1994, it was the best-selling magazine in Japan with a circulation of over six million copies a month.

The Anime Revolution

As noted earlier, animation had barely gotten started in Japan before World War II when it was co-opted by the military and used for propaganda purposes. After the war, except for a few lone cartoonists working on artistic animation projects, there was no animation industry in the country to speak of. A number of artists and animators realized that the only way to produce cartoons or cartoon features was by working together in a studio setting, like Disney, instead of trying to produce cartoons on their own. Still, it took a number of years of hard work to form an actual animation studio.

The first such studio, Toei Animation Co., was organized in 1956. Its earliest leading animator, Yasuji Mori, directed Toei's first important cartoon, *Doodling Kitty*, in May 1957. But it wasn't until the studio released its first full-length theatrical feature, *Panda and the Magic Serpent*, in October 1958 that Toei was recognized as a major player in the cartoon field.

Toei's first few features followed the Disney formula very closely. Each film was produced a year apart, and the stories were based on popular folk tales. The heroes always had a number of cute, funny animal companions. Toei's first six films were distributed in the United States, usually a couple of years after they were first shown in Japan. The second through sixth were *Magic Boy* (1959), *Alakazam the Great* (1960), *The Littlest Warrior* (1961), *The Adventures of Sinbad* (1962), and *The Little Prince and the Eight-Headed Dragon* (1963). Unfortunately, the films didn't make a profit in the United States, and Japanese animated movies vanished from the American screen for the next twenty years.

However, the movie *Alakazam the Great* led to something

unexpected. Although directed by Taiji Yabushita, the film was based upon a popular 1950s manga by Osamu Tezuka that was an adaptation of the ancient Chinese Monkey King legend. Since the movie used Tezuka's plot and visual style, he was consulted on its production and became involved with its promotion. This introduction to the world of film led him to switch his focus from comic books to animation. A lifelong fan of Disney animation, no doubt Tezuka had always harbored a secret desire to produce his own cartoons. And now he had the chance.

Tezuka, like many animators across the world, was strongly influenced by the appearance of the first Hanna-Barbera television cartoons of the late 1950s. These cartoons, done in a very limited animation style, led him to conclude that he could produce similarly limited animation cartoons for the growing TV market. Equally important, he understood, based on the popularity of his comic books—especially such futuristic titles as *Astro Boy*—that there was a strong demand for modern, fast-paced fantasy, which the animation establishment, with its narrow focus on fairy tales, was completely ignoring.

Tezuka soon founded Japan's first TV animation studio, Mushi Productions. Its first major release was a weekly series based upon *Astro Boy*, which debuted on New Year's Day, January 1, 1963. It was an instant success, and by the end of 1963, there were three more television animation studios in production. Plus, Toei Animation opened a special TV animation division. By the end of the 1960s, the popularity of TV science fiction action-adventure anime was so overwhelming that Toei began to alternate it with fairy tale fare for its theatrical features.

Television animation became much more popular in Japan than it ever was in the United States. One possible reason why is that censorship was not as much of a problem in Japan, as children's television was not as heavily monitored as it was in the United States. Tezuka himself had already brought sophisticated adult animation to movie theaters with his 1969 art feature *A Thousand and One Nights*, which included much of the eroticism of the original and his 1970 *Cleopatra*, a time-travel comedy filled with anachronisms, such as Julius Caesar appearing as a cigar-chomping, American-style politician. Tezuka, working on one project after another in the animation and manga field, helped lay the groundwork for the diversity that manga and anime enjoys today.

As Tezuka's success in anime grew, numerous other artists took his basic ideas and added to them, expanding the field in new and exciting directions. Manga continued to flourish, and anime, based on the most popular published manga, did also.

By the 1970s, TV studios such as TCJ (Television Corporation of Japan), Tatsunoko Production Co., Tokyo Movie Shinsha (TMS), and Nippon Animation, among others, were turning out animated mystery dramas, older-teen sports-team soap operas, and classics such as *Heidi, Anne of the Green Gables,* and *The Diary of Anne Frank,* along with traditional juvenile fantasy adventures.

The next ten years was a time of incredible growth for the anime industry. One development that increased the popularity of both manga and anime was the toy business. During the 1970s, toy manufacturers discovered that toys tied in with animated shows sold much better than toys without tie-ins. Few laws governed cross-marketing consumer goods in Japan, and Japanese manufacturers soon became experts at cross-marketing popular anime and manga characters. While product tie-ins were nothing new in the United States (Disney having perfected the concept many years earlier), the extent of cross-marketing and toy promotions carried out in Japan far exceeded anything ever attempted in the United States. Anime became the machine that drove the Japanese toy and novelty market, and, later, the video game market.

TV anime in the 1970s was dominated by the adventures of giant robots. Perhaps the most influential show was Toei's adaptation of comic book artist Go Nagai's *Mazinger Z*. This anime was based on the first of a series of graphic novels about a gigantic flying mechanical warrior controlled by a teenage pilot who uses it to defend Earth against invading space monsters. The story took the concept of brave airplane fighter pilots in combat with enemy armies to a whole new level. *Mazinger Z*—and Nagai's direct sequels *Great Mazinger* and *UFO Robo Grendizer*—ran for 222 weekly episodes from 1972 through 1977.

In a somewhat similar vein was *Space Battleship Yamato* from 1974, with the united Earth armies fighting from planet to planet across the galaxy against the conquering Gamilon invaders. *Yamato* was fortunately timed for the explosive popularity of space operas following the importation of *Star Wars* from the United States; a *Yamato* TV series and theatrical-feature sequels followed. During the late 1970s and early 1980s, the hottest cartoonist in anime was *Yamato*'s creator, Leiji Matsumoto; there were TV cartoon series and theatrical features based upon his other space-adventure manga, such as *Captain Harlock, Galaxy Express 999*, and *Captain Harlock and The Queen of 1,000 Years.*

In 1977, the most important science fiction film of all time, *Star Wars,* opened in Japan. The movie was a huge hit and it influenced in one way or another all manga and anime that followed. Galactic empires, humanoid robots, and sword fights, already staples of anime, received a huge boost from *Star Wars* and its sequels. That influence can still be seen in today's anime.

Further fueling the giant robot/science fiction explosion in the late 1970s was a new series that began in 1979 called *Mobile Suit Gundam.* It combined the epic story elements of *Yamato* with the oversize, humanoid robots of *Mazinger Z. Mobile Suit Gundam* was an intelligent and exciting space opera. The vast story detailed a future space war in which the opposing forces fought each other in mechanized "battle suits." Human pilots actually "wore" the giant robots as a protective shell and battle armor.

Initially a modest hit, *Mobile Suit Gundam* quickly became a nationwide obsession when the series was rerun and later compiled into three theatrical films. One of the factors of the series' success was an extensive line of plastic model kits based on the series' giant robot suits. Soon, new *Gundam* films, videos, and television sequels started to appear.

Within a few years, a huge number of new space operas emerged to take on the *Gundam* franchise. The most notable was *Chojiju Yasai Macross* (shown in the United States as the first third of *Robotech*), which attracted a huge fan base not only in Japan but in the United States as well. Anime was becoming a worldwide phenomenon.

The man most responsible for this phenomenon, Osamu Tezuka, died in early 1989. In 1994, the city of Takarazuka, where Tezuka grew up, opened the Osamu Tezuka Museum of Comic Art. In 1997, the Japanese government issued a series of postage stamps featuring his artwork. He was certainly the most influential artist ever to work in Japan—if not the world.

Anime in the 1980s

After its incredible success in the 1970s, it appeared that anime had no place to go but down. Yet the field in the 1980s confounded its critics by expanding in new and different directions. Anime actually grew even more popular in the 1980s and 1990s as it became a worldwide sensation.

After twenty years of television series, anime returned to the motion picture screen in Japan in the mid-1980s through the efforts of two men: artists Hayao Miyazaki and Isao Takahata.

Hayao Miyazaki got his start in children's manga in the 1960s. In the early 1980s, he wrote an ecology-minded science fiction adventure, *Nausicaa of the Valley of the Wind* for *Animage*, an animation fan magazine published by Tokuma, one of Japan's largest publishers. The story was so popular that Tokuma financed a feature-length animated movie of the story, directed by Miyazaki. *Nausicaa* was a huge hit, and its popularity led Tokuma to finance a new animation company, Studio Ghibli, which primarily produced animated features based on Miyazaki's work and on that of Isao Takahata.

Some of the better-known animated films produced by Studio Ghibli include *Laputa: Castle in the Sky* (1986), *My Neighbor Totoro* (1988), *Kiki's Delivery Service* (1989), and Takahata's *Grave of the Fireflies* (1988). In a major deal with Disney Studios signed in 1996 Ghibli agreed to release all of its major animated films in the United States with dubbed voices, under the Disney banner. So far, every Ghibli film has been a hit in the video marketplace.

Another breakthrough directly affecting anime took place in the early 1980s with the debut of a new style of science fiction. It was in the writings of authors William Gibson, Bruce Sterling, and Neal Stephenson that cyberpunk was born. This new style of storytelling featured jagged-edge fiction about a near future in which hackers and crackers and web-heads roam the dark corridors of virtual reality in cyberspace. The cyberpunk revolution was further defined by Ridley Scott's dystopian view of the future in his 1982 film *Blade Runner*.

Quick to react to this new version of reality were Japanese manga and anime artists. The first cyberpunk anime was *Akira*, in 1988, written and directed by Katsuhiro Otomo. A near-future epic dealing with mutant children living in a harsh, technopop Neo-Tokyo, the movie was one of the most expensive anime films ever made. On initial release in Japan, it was a flop. However, the film was a major hit outside Japan and helped establish anime as the medium for cutting-edge science fiction storytelling.

Working in a similar vein was artist Masamune Shirow. His adaptation of his original manga *Appleseed* to anime presented a future where the line between machine and human was beginning to blur. It was a topic he dealt with in even greater depth with his 1995 film *Ghost in the Shell*, which was later re-imagined as an anime TV series.

Cyberpunk remains a potent force in science fiction and anime. However, much of its impact has been muted by a present that is evolving as quickly as any science fiction story, but in totally unexpected and unforeseen directions. Not even anime can keep up with today's changing world of technology.

Another important change in the anime field that occurred in the 1980s was the development of Original Anime Videos (OAVs). Starting in 1984, studios began producing animation for direct sale to customers, completely bypassing television and movie release. These new videos were called Original Anime Videos by Japanese anime fans—a name that has since made its way across the ocean. OAV animation is usually of better quality than TV animation, but not as visually detailed as theatrical animation.

OAVs also often feature stories that are too long for a standard theatrical release, but not long enough to make up a TV series. OAVs can run from a half hour to two hours in length, and from one video to independent series that extend over two or more tapes. Since the OAV market is not subject to the usual film and TV guidelines for bad taste or violence, they often feature both in excessive amounts. However, some of the better OAV productions, such as the *PatLabor* near-future police-procedural dramas or the *No Time for Tenchi* teen sci-fi comedies, have become so popular they have led to their own anime TV series and theatrical films.

Anime Today

Anime in the 1990s continued to entertain children and young adults throughout the world. The amazing successes of *Sailor Moon, Dragonball Z,* and *Pokémon* surprised even their creators and propelled anime to the front ranks of children's entertainment in the United States.

Unfortunately, a number of unpredicted events in the mid-1990s rocked the anime world and caused deep divisions among the followers of anime throughout Japan and the world.

Perhaps the most controversial and overanalyzed series in all of anime debuted in 1995. Directed by Hideaki Anno, the show was titled *Neon Genesis Evangelion*. Originally, the anime seemed like any other giant-robots-save-the-Earth-from-mysterious-invaders story, but the plot soon turned dark and depressing and was filled with psychiatric and religious references points. Several groups on Earth plotted against each other while battling alien invaders called Angels who had their own plans for humanity. With its startling sexual images, continual references to psychology, and obscure allusions to Christian theology, *Neon Genesis Evangelion* succeeded in being one of the first anime shows that had fans arguing over the meaning of each episode. With its confused religious messages and overt sexuality, *Neon Genesis Evangelion* also succeeded in becoming the first anime ever censored by Tokyo TV. The story line proved so controversial that Hideaki Anno wrote (and produced) several different conclusions to the story, none of which completely satisfied any group of fans.

Many devoted anime fans viewed *Neon Genesis Evangelion* as a major step forward in anime, a blending of important and meaningful story with deep and rich cultural reference points. Other fans, equally vocal and equally devoted, saw the show as pretentious, boring, and superficial. Written during a period when Hideaki Anno was suffering from deep depression, the series, they felt, was nothing more than the director's attempt to rationalize his unsettled state of mind. The show supports both lines of reasoning, and its impact on recent Japanese cartooning cannot be ignored.

Not as controversial, the series *Cowboy Bebop* was also censored by the Japanese television networks due to its unrelenting and prophetic violence. Shortly after the September 11, 2001, hijacking of several airplanes in the United States that were flown into the World Trade Center towers in New York City, a *Cowboy Bebop* episode dealt with planes being hijacked by terrorists in Japan. Due to the remarkable similarity to real life, the episode was never shown on Japanese TV. Several other *Cowboy Bebop* episodes were also censored in both Japan and the United States due to excessive and realistic violence. Still, complete collections of all the shows in the series have continued to sell well on DVD.

The Aum Shinrikyo cult sarin-gas attacks on the Japanese subway system in 1995 were a major disaster for anime fans. Because the cult had ties with pop culture, ordinary people on the street were quick to blame media and anime fans for the horrific results. The situation was much like that of the United States in the late 1950s, when the Senate tried to blame the rise in juvenile delinquency on kids reading comic books. For a few months, anime fans found themselves being blamed for many of the ills in Japanese culture. Fortunately, as more was learned about the cult, its ties with anime were mostly discredited and fans were no longer seen as monsters in human form.

As anime enters one step at a time into the twenty-first century, it remains one of the most important forms of modern entertainment. It's an art form that is popular all over the world, and the characters who inhabit its many worlds are as well known as the Disney cartoon heroes of a previous generation. Manga and anime continue to succeed due to the hard work of the artists and writers involved in the stories. It is their commitment to quality that has made the field one of the leading sources of entertainment for children, teens, and adults today. It is a field that deals with new ideas and welcomes challenge and change. Anime is, essentially, a look at possible futures. As such, it is the perfect arena for the introduction of new scientific principles and concepts —ideas that we explore in the rest of this book.

2. Mecha

The World of Giant Robots

One of the most significant aspects of anime is the incorporation of *mecha,* or giant robots, into plots and entire series that span decades. These giant robots are often driven by children and teenagers, either by remote control or by neural transmissions. Often, the survival of the world is at stake, and all will be lost if the mecha don't save the day. In other series, the mecha battle each other: good versus evil, with strength dominating for one side or the other. While the earliest mecha consisted of elaborate "battle suits" and Transformer-like capabilities, more modern mecha incorporate complex prosthetics, artificial intelligence, and biotechnology.

In this chapter, we take a close look at mecha: what the term really means, how it has evolved in anime over the decades, the state of mecha in anime today, and the evolution of real robotics. We'll tell you the difference between automatons, androids, and robots, and explain how the concept of mecha borrows from all three. And most importantly, we'll look at the anime itself: everything from *Gigantor* in the early 1960s to more modern shows such as *Texhnolyze, New Getter Robo, Metropolis,* and *Mobile Suit Gundam SEED,* to name only a few of the dozens of anime series this chapter discusses.

In the world of anime, mecha refers to gigantic humanoid robots and human-piloted robotic vehicles. Some mecha look like people, others look like animals, and still others look like huge robotic fighting machines. While real robots usually operate autonomously or by remote control, anime mecha often have human pilots. Most mecha are built for war. Smaller mecha are basically powered suits of, and while they are similar to larger human-piloted mecha in many ways, they are worn rather than piloted.

Powered suits of armor are generally exoskeletons that protect the wearers during battle. The suits are very heavy, so they come with self-powering units of some kind; an example might be hydraulic power to lift the suits and give the wearers increased mobility. Space suits are an elementary real-world example of powered suits (that aren't equipped with built-in weapons). In *Bubblegum Crisis,* to name one anime that features extensive use of powered armor suits, vigilante women wear mechanized armor. The Mechs in the games BattleTech and Mechwarrior also rely heavily on powered armor. And in the related field of comic books, Marvel Comics' Iron Man wears a powered armor suit to help him fight evil; Doctor Doom wears a powered armor suit to help him fight good.

Mecha are very popular both in manga and anime, and in Western countries, mecha are common gaming devices—such as in the popular strategy game BattleTech, which has spawned numerous computer and role-playing games. In fact, some people suggest that BattleTech is where the term mecha was first used, probably because of the BattleMechs, or robotic humanoid battle giants.

The average anime mecha is about twenty feet (or more) tall and comes with lots of weapons strapped on. The average mecha pilot is a young teenager, and usually, the pilot is a guy—though not always. Some mecha are like Transformers and can change appearance and operation; Macross is one example. Other mecha, such as Voltron, merge to form even bigger mecha. While it may seem as if Transformers and Macross were the earliest versions of this kind of mecha, it's generally thought that Go Nagai invented the form in 1974 with the creation of Getter Robo.

The term mecha also has to do with mechanical engineering, of course. In fact, the term mechatronics, which denotes the study of automata, or robotic/mechanical devices, combines mecha (mechanical engineering) with tronics (electronics). An automaton is a device that moves autonomously; a mecha is an automaton.

Czech playwright Karel Capek coined the word *robot* to refer to the forced labor of serfs; the Czechoslovak word for "work" happens to be *robota,* and indeed, when Czechoslovakia was a feudal nation, robota were the peasants who were forced to farm the noblemen's lands for free. In Capek's 1921 play *RUR (Rossum's Universal Robots),* an Englishman named Rossum mass-produces automata that will do the work of humans, hence giving humans more free time for intellectual, spiritual, and emotional pursuits. It was new then, though it's old now: the automata wanted to start their own race of intelligent life and take over the world, killing all humans. The play was very popular, and people starting using the word robot rather than automaton, though both words denote the same thing. (It's interesting to note that Capek's robots were not mechanical; instead, they were created by chemicals, and were thus more along the lines of traditional androids, which are robotic beings created in some biological or chemical way.) These days, a robot is generally considered a computerized/mechanical device that does tasks that humans used to do. Clearly, the line between robot and mecha is thin.

History and Evolution of Anime Mecha

Capek claimed that he wanted to call his automatons "labors," and that his brother Josef suggested the word "robot." In Japan, *RUR* was staged in 1923. The play generated worldwide interest in automata, robots, and mecha.

Then, in 1926, Fritz Lang's movie *Metropolis* was released; it arrived in Japan in 1929. Many people point to *Metropolis* as the movie that launched modern robotics research. The robot in the film, Maria, was female, cold, and metallic.

Much later, in around 1952, Osamu Tezuka created the manga/animation called *Tetsuwan Atomu.* The hero of the manga/animation, Tetsuwan Atomu, was a "little boy" robot, and the point of the series was that technology can enable humankind to do either good or evil in the world. Atomu was powered by nuclear energy and had the heart of his inventor's son. In some respects he was an offshoot of World War II's nuclear disaster, yet he had a human heart, showing that humankind can use technology for good if we so choose. Because he was very small, Atomu bore little resemblance to the powered armor suits and gigantic mecha that would follow him. Of course, Atomu did battle gigantic machines, as do most (if not all) mecha.

A 1960s manga/animation called *Tetsujin 28* (aka *Gigantor*) featured a giant robot that is operated by a little boy using a remote control. *Tetsu* means *metal* in Japanese, so both *Tetsuwan* and *Tetsujin* refer to their metal main characters.

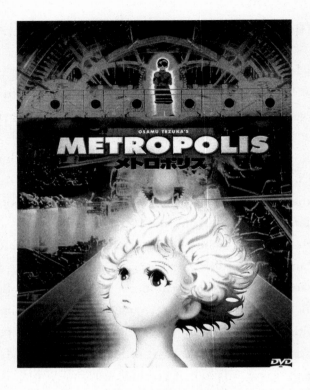

Meanwhile, in the real world, Kawasaki Heavy Industries released its Unimate industrial robot in 1969. We mark the Unimate in our anime mecha timeline because it was the beginning of heavy Japanese involvement in industrial robotics development.

Following on the heels of Unimate came the *Mazinger Z* anime in 1973. *Mazinger Z* featured a round, humanlike robot that was more than just a war machine. For the first time, a pilot was inside the mecha; in this case, the pilot had a tiny airplane that he docked inside the robot's head to use as the robot's brain.

Also in 1973, the Wabot-1 robot was released by the Atsuo Takanishi Laboratory at Waseda University. The Wabot was the first Japanese humanoid robot. It couldn't walk, but it could shift weight from one leg to the other, simulating a clumsy sort of gait. It also had primitive speech and visual processing functions.

In 1979 we find ourselves at the beginning of the mecha boom period. This is when *Mobile Suit Gundam* first appeared. For years in Japanese anime, giant robots had been fighting alone against outer space aliens. Now, for the first time, these giant robots were in armies, and they were mass-produced. Rather than one pilot in a mecha trying to save the world against outer space invasions, *Gundam* gave fans a complex story about human space colonies fighting a vast war of independence. *Gundam* robots were complicated machines, and each type had specialized abilities and functions. We discuss the plot of *Mobile Suit Gundam* in greater detail later on in this book.

By 1980, the mecha boom was in full force. In the real world at that date, Japan had more industrial robots than any other country. In fact, it's been estimated that 50 percent of all the robots in the world were in Japan at that time.

Early in the 1980s, *Macross* followed *Gundam*'s lead and gave fans a story in which mass-produced robots live on another planet. The *Macross* robots are able to transform themselves into other robotic machines. A race of giant aliens threatens humanity, and the giant *Macross* robots must battle the aliens to save humankind. Later, American producer Carl Macek bought *Macross,* along with two other Japanese anime, *Super Dimension Cavalry Southern Cross* and *Genesis Climber Mospeada*. Out of these, Macek created one of the most significant mecha anime of all time: *Robotech*.

Armored Trooper Votoms was another mecha anime from the early 1980s, and it featured centuries-long wars among people living in a far-off galaxy. The Votoms were true war machines. In the real world, by 1986, Honda had produced its P-0 mechanical pair of legs. This was a step toward creating humanoid robots that could walk. Anime robots continued to evolve, as well: In 1988, an anime called *Mobile Police Patlabor* was released, and its robots were mass-produced for use as tools, law-enforcement machines, and exploration vehicles. These robots were artificially intelligent, and the people lived on a planet just like Earth rather than on a space colony in a distant galaxy. There were no wars in *Patlabor*. The mecha were not giant robot fighting machines. This may have been a turning point in the anime mecha subgenre.

In 1993, Honda's P-1 was released, and it was a true *walking* humanoid robot. It also had two moving arms. But the world of anime had to wait two more years for *its* next major generation of robots.

That's when the phenomenal *Neon Genesis Evangelion* arrived. This anime marked a major evolution in the genre. It posed philosophical, ethical, and moral questions regarding robots. Why do they exist? Who created them, and for what purpose? Why do robots fight? Are they "real" or just "machines"? *Evangelion* involved far more than a simple plot about armored machines fighting aliens on another planet. Rather, it was a complex mixture of machines, religion, and biology. In this anime, the robots are armored living creatures who evolved from the remains of the first Angel, called Adam. These robots were created to prevent the Angels from destroying the world. Specially selected pilots control the robots using the human brain and nervous system. The robots themselves are created by NERV, an organization that's fighting the Angels. It's a biotechnology twist in high gear. Again, we discuss *Neon Genesis Evangelion* in greater detail further on in this book.

In 1996, Honda released its first autonomous robot, the P-2. This unit didn't need external power or control. Then, in 1999, Sony's AIBO showed up: a domestic robot in the shape of an artificially intelligent dog. It was followed in 2000 by Honda's ASIMO, which operates light switches and door knobs, sits in a chair, moves freely in a human living environment, and communicates "intelligently" with humans.

During this time, many other mecha anime were released, including *Gasaraki, Big O, Metropolis, Mahoromatic, RahXephon, Texhnolyze,* and of course, all the *Gundams.* All will be discussed a little later in the book.

Anime Mecha: The Shows

One of the earliest mecha anime on the scene was known as *Gigantor,* or *Tetsujin 28,* which means Iron Man 28 in Japanese. The first

Gigantor series had eighty-three episodes and ran from 1963 through 1965. The second series had thirteen episodes and ran from 1965 through 1966. And a color sequel to the original *Tetsujin 28* aired in 1980–81. Not all episodes were translated into English.

In *Gigantor,* twelve-year-old Jimmy Sparks remotely controls an enormous robot to fight worldwide crime. The anime is set in the year 2000, and given that it aired in the early to mid-1960s, its robot is like a toy of its time grown to gigantic proportions. Gigantor, the robot, is made out of steel with eyes that never move; he has a rocket-powered backpack that enables him to fly. Gigantor has no artificial intelligence whatsoever, but he is incredibly strong. In the episode called "Dangerous Dinosaurs," Gigantor needs repairs when he loses an arm and a leg; otherwise, throughout the series, he seems indestructible. Jimmy Sparks has an unusual life. Not only does he have Gigantor, but he lives on an isolated island with his uncle, Dr. Bob Brilliant, and always carries a gun, just in case Gigantor fails to save the day.

On the steel heels of Gigantor came other mecha anime, such as *Mazinger Z* in 1973. In this series, Dr. Hell and his army of mechanical monsters threaten humanity from the island of Bardos in the Aegean Sea. The only thing standing between Dr. Hell and the survival of humankind is Mazinger Z, a gigantic (of course!) robot made out of *chogokin,* an indestructible metal. (Are you starting to see a pattern?) Unlike Gigantor, Mazinger Z has plenty of advanced weapons to help him battle humanity's foes. But like Gigantor, Mazinger Z has a young boy pilot; in Mazinger Z's case, the pilot is the hot-headed teenager Kouji Kabuto.

Kouji's grandfather, scientist Dr. Kabuto, created Mazinger Z to protect humanity from Dr. Hell. But then Dr. Hell's henchman, Baron Ashura, kills Kouji's grandfather, and so Kouji sets out to use Mazinger Z to avenge his grandfather's death and save the world. Many fans have long considered *Mazinger Z* to be the first major mecha anime, the one that created the entire subgenre. And its creator, Go Nagai, is famous in anime circles.

In 1974, *Getter Robo* appeared—and was followed by all sorts of Robo shows, such as the *Great Mazinger tai Getter Robo* movie, *Getter Robo G, Great Mazinger tai Getter Robo G, Getter Robo Go, Getter Robo: Armageddon, Shin Getter Robo, Neo Getter Robo,* and others. *Getter Robo* itself, the first series, brings dinosaurs onto Earth with the usual demonic motive: to wipe out all humans. These dinosaurs rise from the bowels of the planet, and they happen to be mechanical dinosaurs created by real, living dinosaurs dwelling beneath Earth's surface.

While we think it's unlikely that real dinosaurs live beneath Earth and have the intelligence and capability to create an army of mechanical dinosaurs, we acknowledge the template from which the plot is drawn. From the beginning of film, we've had King Kong and Godzilla, and Hercules battling all sorts of monsters. Perhaps the interesting difference is that, in *Getter Robo,* the monsters are mechanical in nature. And thus, when Getter Robo, the good guy, battles the monsters, we witness one of the first clashes of robots versus robots. The Saotome Research Institute sends Getter Robo into battle along with his pilots: Ryo Nagare, martial arts expert Musashi Tomoe, and the unpopular Hayato Jin.

And now we move to a series of monumental importance in anime history: *Mobile Suit Gundam*, 1979. Of all mecha anime, *Mobile Suit Gundam* reigns as king. Though initially a failure (as was *Star Trek*, according to its television ratings), the first *Gundam* series eventually became so popular that it spawned many other *Gundam* spin-off series and movies. We'll give you a quick rundown here, then talk about the mecha in some of the spin-off series later in this chapter:

- *Mobile Suit Gundam*, 1979, 43 episodes
- *Gundam 1*, 1981, movie
- *Gundam II: Soldiers of Sorrow*, 1981, movie
- *Gundam III: Encounters in Space*, 1982, movie
- *Mobile Suit Zeta Gundam*, 1985, 50 episodes
- *Mobile Suit Gundam ZZ*, 1986, 47 episodes
- *Gundam: Char's Counterattack*, 1988, movie
- *Gundam 0080: War in the Pocket*, 1989, 6 episodes
- *Mobile Suit Gundam F91*, 1991, movie
- *Gundam 0083: Stardust Memory*, 1991, 13 episodes
- *Gundam 0083: Last Blitz of Zeon*, 1992, movie
- *Mobile Suit Victory Gundam*, 1993, 51 episodes
- *Mobile Fighter G Gundam*, 1994, 49 episodes
- *New Mobile Report Gundam W*, 1995, 49 episodes

- *Gundam M.S.: The 08th Team,* 1996, 12 episodes
- *After War Gundam X,* 1996, 39 episodes
- *Mobile Suit Gundam Wing: Endless Waltz,* 1997, 3 episodes
- *Gundam M.S.: The 08th Team: Miller's Report,* 1998, movie
- *Gundam Wing: Endless Waltz,* 1998, movie
- *Gundam,* 1999, 50 episodes
- *G-Saviour,* 2000 movie
- *Gundam Evolve,* 2001, 12 episodes
- *Green Divers,* 2001, movie
- *Gundam: Earth Light,* 2002, movie
- *Gundam: Moonlight Butterfly,* 2002, movie
- *Mobile Suit Gundam SEED,* 2002, 50 episodes
- *Gundam SEED Special Edition,* 2004, 6 episodes
- *Gundam SEED DESTINY,* 2004, approximately 50 episodes
- *Zeta Gundam I: Heirs to the Stars,* 2004, movie
- *Zeta Gundam II,* 2005, movie
- *Zeta Gundam III,* 2006, movie

As you can see, we could easily fill this entire book with nothing but information about *Gundam.* And even though *Gundam* began so long ago—in 1979—there are yet more new *Gundam* shows and movies on the horizon.

Why was *Mobile Suit Gundam* so popular? Why have fans been fascinated with this mecha anime for so many years? The simple answer is that *Gundam* is the epitome of mecha anime. With complex story lines, settings that are not on Earth, and a wide variety of fighting robots, *Gundam* marks a major forward thrust in anime.

Much of the *Gundam* saga takes place on what is called the Universal Century timeline. According to the story, because Earth is overcrowded, humans have started a space-colonization program, and after living away from Earth for decades, the people in space (about 80 percent of all humans) want their independence from the people on Earth. In U.C. 0079, the Principality of Zeon goes to war against the Earth Federation. This war becomes known as the One Year War.

Zeon plans to attack Federation Forces headquarters in South America, but instead destroys Sydney, Australia. More than four billion Earth people die within the first week of the war against Zeon, which is using nuclear weapons. Then the Earth Federation and Zeon sign the Antarctic Treaty. All weapons of mass destruction are now against the law.

In the One Year War, Zeon pilots wear mobile suits rather than fly airplanes. These mobile suits provide all weapons and shields, in addition to flight and underwater capabilities. Eventually, the Earth Federation creates its own mobile suits, but the Federation's research and development takes place on a space colony, which Zeon attacks and overwhelms. The Zeon conquest puts the Federation's new mobile suit technology into enemy hands.

A young boy named Amuro Ray must pilot a Federation RX-78

white mobile suit called Gundam. The Gundam is the most successful of three prototype mobile suits created by the Federation. It is made of "Luna Titanium" armor and incorporates beam rifles and beam sabers, as well as a computer system that enables the mobile suit to learn from its human pilot. Eventually, the Gundam will be able to function without a human pilot. It will possess keen artificial intelligence. Luckily for Earth, Amuro Ray is a terrific Gundam pilot, and the mobile suit Gundam blows away any Zeon weapon that attacks it.

Notice the advance of science in *Mobile Suit Gundam*, especially in contrast to the robotics in the earlier *Mazinger Z* and *Gigantor* series. The Gundam has the ability to learn. It uses advanced computer systems. It's something beyond a fighting robot with no brain. The mobile suit itself is approximately ten times taller than an average man. The pilot sits in a cockpit in the mobile suit's chest.

After Amuro Ray and his Gundam destroy two Zaku mobile suits from Zeon, the Federation ship White Base leaves the Side 7 space colony (Amuro's home planet). Onboard the White Base are the other prototype mobile suits, along with a bunch of refugees. The White Base heads toward the Federation's headquarters in South America. But as the White Base nears Earth, Zeon commander Char Aznable attacks the Federation ship, and the White Base veers away from South America and ends up landing in Zeon territory in North America.

And now the plot thickens. Char's friend Garma Zabi is the

youngest son of Zeon's ruler, Degwin Zabi. Garma Zabi happens to be the commander of Zeon's Earthbound armies, and so it's natural that Char enlists his friend's help in defeating the White Base. But sadly for Char, he unwittingly leads his friend to his death at the hands of the White Base. Degwin Zabi is extremely upset that his son is dead. Char is removed from his position, but Kycilia, who is Degwin Zabi's daughter, takes Char into her own service.

In the meantime, Dozle Zabi, another son, sends off one of Zeon's best pilots, Ramba Ral, to take revenge by finding and destroying the White Base.

We weren't kidding when we told you that, with *Mobile Suit Gundam*, mecha anime evolved into a more sophisticated art form, with complex timelines, battles, stories, and fleets of computerized, specialized combat robots. (And keep in mind that we're giving you only a bare-bones idea of the *Mobile Suit Gundam* saga. It's far more complex than the outline provided here.)

The White Base escapes from North America and joins Operation Odessa, which is a Federation maneuver intent on taking over Zeon's resource mines in central Asia. Not only does the White Base have to fend off assaults from Ramba Ral, it must now fight off attacks from Zeon's Black Tri-Stars team. These Black Tri-Stars are Zeon's best mobile-suit pilots, and they use a "jetstream attack," which means they line up and attack at top speed, one after the other, either in space or on the ground.

Eventually, the White Base emerges from battle and continues on to Ireland, and from there to South America. Char is now commanding a submarine squadron of mobile suits for Zeon.

In South America, the Federation is mass-producing mobile suits on an underground base. These mobile suits are based, of course, on the original RX-78 Gundam and are called RGM-79 GM suits. The RGM-79 GM mobile suits are not made from Luna Titanium, and have short-range beam spray guns rather than beam rifles.

Later, as the Federation ramps up to attack a Zeon space fortress, its fleet is attacked by a new Zeon mobile armor known as the MAN-08 Elmeth. Weighing 164 tons, the MAN-08 has remote-controlled wireless weapons, each with mega particle cannons, sensors, and rocket thrusters. "Mega particle cannon" is another term for "beam weapon," and in the technobabble of *Mobile Suit Gundam,* it's created by the compression of "positive and negative Minovsky particles," which are subatomic particles discovered by scientist Y. T. Minovsky.

These particles have either positive or negative charges, and in open space, they interfere with communications and computer circuits. They cannot be detected by radar or long-range wireless communications. Because they destroy electronics and communications equipment, they must incorporate shielding. In addition, Minovsky particles arrange themselves into three-dimensional cubic lattices, and hence, function as force fields, which are called I-fields in the *Mobile Suit Gundam* world. When lattices are compressed, they create neutral mega particles, which can be turned into massive energy beams.

The mega particle cannon, or beam rifle, of the MAN-08 Elmeth becomes standard equipment in mobile suits. The cannon's energy comes from an energy capacitor, or E-CAP, which stores the Minovsky particles in a compressed state.

The MAN-08 Elmeth is piloted by a Newtype, or a human who has evolved with amazing amounts of intuition, awareness, and overall ability to predict the immediate future. Eventually Newtypes are considered to be living weapons. They are able to transmit and receive "psycho-waves," or thoughts. They use psycho-waves to communicate with machines, and they can read the minds of lesser humans. We'll talk about the man-machine interface more in chapter 3.

If the MAN-08 Elmeth and its Minovsky particles don't sound futuristic enough, Zeon's ultimate weapon at this point in *Mobile Suit Gundam* turns out to be a Solar Ray laser cannon. The Solar Ray is an entire space colony that has been converted into a laser cannon. It can be used only once. After all, if you turn an entire space colony into a laser cannon, the space colony is *gone*.

Some of the Federation's mecha in *Mobile Suit Gundam* are:

Gundam: 60 tons, 18 meters tall, equipped with vulcan gun (multibarreled machine gun), two beam sabers (works with Minovsky particles and E-CAPS, but a saber rather than a rifle), two beam rifles (mega particle cannons), a hyper bazooka (giant rocket launcher), and other weapons.

Guncannon: another of the three mobile suit prototypes created when the Federation introduced the Gundam; 70 tons, about 18 meters tall, equipped with vulcan gun, two cannons, and two beam rifles.

Guntank: the last of the three mobile suit prototypes created when the Federation introduced the Gundam; 56 tons, 15 meters tall, equipped with a cannon and two quadruple missile launchers; has no legs, no hands; used for long-range artillery fire.

Ball: mass-produced pod armed with a cannon, 17 tons, 12 meters tall.

And on the side of Zeon, we have a lot of mecha, some of which are:

Char's Zaku II: 56 tons, 18 meters tall, equipped with machine gun, bazooka, and optional heat hawk (an axe with thermal energy); the standard Zaku II is mass-produced by Zeon and nearly destroys Earth's population. Operates in space, on land, and in water. No match, however, for the Mobile Suit Gundam.

Gouf: operates on land, equipped with finger machine guns, defensive shield, and electric whip, optional heat saber.

Dom: operates on land but has legs with jet engines so it can turn into a hovercraft.

Rick Dom: a Dom with rockets instead of jet engines in the legs; comes with a mighty bazooka and weighs close to 80 tons.

Gelgoog: almost as mighty as the Gundam!

Gogg: thick-bodied, mass-produced amphibious mobile suit;

equipped with mega particle cannon, two torpedo launchers, two iron nails.

Acguy: another amphibious mobile suit; right arm has mega particle cannon, left arm has rocket launchers, weighs 92 tons, stands 19 meters tall; equipped with a total of four rocket launchers and six mega particle cannons.

Z'gok: highly advanced amphibious mobile suit with 360-degree "mono-eye sensor" (looks like the eye of a Cyclops; is an optical camera with laser and infra-red sensors).

Bigro: used in outer space warfare, weighs close to 126 tons, equipped with mega particle cannon, eight missile launchers.

Braw Bro: a Newtype mobile suit, has a "psycommu" man-machine interface, mega particle cannons.

Zeong: another Newtype mobile suit with a psycommu system.

Big Zam: equipped with 28 mega particle cannons, an I-field barrier that deflects all beam weapons; weighs 1,021 tons.

Following the gigantic leap in anime technology made by *Mobile Suit Gundam, Macross* in 1984 offered more space battles among robots, more transforming robots, and more complex plots. *Macross* is considered a classic of mecha anime and is very similar to *Gundam*. But in *Macross*, viewers were bombarded by antiwar messages. *Macross* plugged a strand of basic human empathy into the notion of giant-robot warfare.

The American version of *Macross* somehow got merged with two other anime series, *Super Dimension Cavalry Southern Cross* and *Genesis Climber Mospeada*. Literally merged. Scenes were actually spliced together from the three series. This new *Macross* transformed itself into a phenomenon called *Robotech*.

Macross takes place during World War III—circa 1999, oddly enough. An alien spaceship crashes into an Earth island called Macross. World War III stops, as humans work together to create a worldwide space navy. The fear is that aliens will attack Earth and try to retrieve their crashed ship. Humans re-create the alien ship, calling the new craft Super Dimensional Fortress One. As predicted, the aliens come to Earth and attack.

Macross/Robotech, like *Gundam*, features space wars and battles between giant transforming robots. For example, the SDF-1

human "motherspace" vessel is a gigantic transforming mecha with a battleship form and a humanoid form. If you've seen the anime, you know that SDF-1 looks like the Transformer toys kids played with in the 1980s. SDF-1 stands on two thick, transforming legs, wields two strong, transforming arms, and is equipped with various weapons. At 1,210 meters tall, it's much taller than the mecha in *Mobile Suit Gundam.*

In addition to the original *Macross* series, many spin-offs were created, among them, *Macross: Do You Remember Love?* in 1984; *Macross Flash Back 2012* in 1987; *Macross II* during 1992; *Macross Plus* in 1994; *Macross Zero* in 2002; and others.

The American version, *Robotech,* ran eighty-five episodes, and, as mentioned, spliced together scenes from three Japanese anime, including *Macross.* As with *Macross,* an alien ship crashes on Earth during World War III, and Earth's governments halt the war to investigate the technology of the alien craft. In the second part of *Robotech,* the children of the original saga must defend Earth while their parents head into space to find the alien home world. In the third and final part, the parents return to Earth, where they discover that the aliens have conquered the planet; the parents battle the aliens to free Earth.

In *Robotech,* alien scientist Zor invents a new form of energy called Protoculture. The rulers of Zor's universe are called Robotech Masters and they control a vast interstellar empire. The Robotech Masters become corrupt and start using Zor's inventions for ill gain. Zor builds a giant space fortress and hides his

Protoculture Factory in the fortress's engines. The factory guarantees unlimited Protoculture for centuries, and Zor sets off into outer space to seed other worlds with the plant from which he extracted Protoculture. But Zor dies on another world, and his disciples launch his space fortress into the universe. The fortress emerges from hyperspace and crashes to Earth.

Of slightly less fame in the mecha anime subgenre, *Armored Trooper Votoms* (circa 1983) featured another series of enormous transforming battle robots that are human-operated and as big as tanks. Votom stands for Vertical One-man Tank for Offense and Maneuvers. As with *Gundam* and *Macross/Robotech*, *Votoms* gave viewers a huge galactic war, this one between the Gilgamesh and Balarant governments. The giant mecha battle in space, in caves, in cities, jungles, rivers: just about anywhere you can imagine. The machines are equipped, variously, with Teh M-09 StereoScope Customs' dual sensors; pulse-Doppler radar; swamp clogs with gliding wheels; torso-mounted cannons; mission computers to handle space flight; rocket boosters; and other equipment. Descent pods drop mecha onto a planet's surface if the atmosphere is too thin for parachutes. These pods feature engines, fuel tanks, and landing skids. A mecha stands on the pod while it descends to the ground.

Basically, up to this point in the mecha anime genre, the stories generally feature gigantic transforming robots in battle. Various science fiction elements are used, including space wars, hyperspace travel, new forms of energy, and all sorts of military weapons and armor. But even aside from the major series, other anime in the early years also feature giant mecha.

One example is *Gunbuster* (1988), which features a young girl who wants to pilot a massive robot called Gunbuster. This anime takes place in 2023, and the girl, Noriko Takaya, must battle huge, insectoid aliens who want to eradicate the human race.

A new twist appears in 1989's *Cybernetics Guardian*, in which an accident releases a demonic spirit in John Stalker, a research pilot for Central Guard Company. Stalker turns into Saldo, a metal cyber-beast consumed by hate. It so happens that Stalker was doing research on a new suit that was supposed to help people in the violent slum known as Cancer. And it also comes out that many years ago, Stalker and other young boys were implanted with seeds of hatred that would enable demonic creatures to come to life later on in the boys' lives. The seeds of hate merge with a strange metal called Astenite to create Devil Armors, the cyber-beasts who work for their evil god, Voldo. While the anime features giant robotlike creatures, the science is weaker than in traditional mecha anime. Demon seeds and strange metals are not as realistic, at least in terms of science, as robots, computers, rocket launchers, and armor.

Starting in 1990 and continuing through 2000, a series of eight different anime called *Brave Saga* brought another bunch of transforming mecha to anime. These shows didn't push the subgenre any further into the future, however. Although unified by the name *Brave Saga,* these eight series were not tied together by a unifying plot. But each featured huge super robots in battle. The shows included *Brave Exkaiser* (48 episodes, 1990), *Brave of the Sun Fightbird* (1991, 48 episodes), *Legendary Brave Da Garn* (1992, 46 episodes), and *Brave Express Might Gaine* (1993, 47 episodes), among others.

In 1992, *Giant Robo* appeared, and again, while the anime features huge super robots in battle, nothing particularly new happens in terms of advancing the mecha subgenre. The plot: Dr. Shizuma invents the Shizuma drive, a new form of energy. A secret organization called Big Fire wants to take over the world and obtains two of the three samples of the Shizuma drive. Dr. Shizuma, along with Giant Robo and the Experts of Justice, battle Big Fire to save the world.

Next up is 1994's *Mobile Suit Fighter G Gundam*, a return to the major series we talked about earlier, *Mobile Suit Gundam*. In this anime, humans live in space colonies that orbit the Earth, and every four years, the ruling nation of the colonies is determined by a battle tournament. Each country sends a mecha Gundam to the match.

In this series some new giant robots appear, among them:

JDG-00x Dark Gundam: built from nanotechnology and capable of self-replication, self-evolution, and self-recovery. In fact, Dark Gundam was formed by the self-replication of Ultimate Gundam, not as evil as Dark Gundam, which infects the dueling Gundam Fighters with biomechanical DG Cells (microscopic nanomachines that are biomechanical viruses; they cover the victim's skin with metallic scales, infect the brain, and turn the victim into a brain-dead but living puppet, and also infect all sorts of machines and vehicles, including other Gundams).

GF13-026ND Mermaid Gundam: an amphibious fighter from Neo-Denmark; invincible in water, transforms into Fisherman Mode to launch high-speed attacks beneath the sea.

GF13-041NSI Ashura Gundam: with six battle arms, hailing from Neo-Singapore; torso and legs separate into three attack units, each with its own set of two arms. The torso unit has built-in missile launchers, and three torso units operating at the same time can launch a lightning-hurling tornado at enemies.

GF13-044NNP Mandala Gundam: the waist and arms look like beads; in fact, this entire Gundam looks like a jack-in-the-box toy. The body is attached to a bell-shaped base, and the Gundam can retract its entire body into the bell, entering Defense Mode. The only weapon this Gundam has is a staff that includes a flame thrower and a beam saber.

GF13-066NO Hurricane Gundam: what can we say? This Gundam disguised itself as a windmill for eleven months to avoid battle. Its main weapon is the Nether Typhoon generated by the windmill on its chest. It also has some beam cannons, but they're peripheral to the normal operations of Hurricane Gundam. The windmill serves as a propeller when the Gundam is in airborne Flight Mode.

GF13-002NGR Zeus Gundam: from Neo-Greece, piloted by the gigantic Marcelot Chronos; this Gundam has large wings that enable it to soar like an eagle, and the mecha rides into battle on a chariot, calling for the Lightning of Judgment, which then hurls down from the sky and kills opponents by thunderbolt.

This is only a partial list; there are many more, including Spike Gundam and Arachno Gundam.

The big changes in these mecha are the nanotech and biomech capabilities of units such as the Dark Gundam. After the 1994 *Mobile Suit Fighter G Gundam* series came *Mobile Suit Gundam Wing* in 1995–1996. Once again, the *Mobile Suit Gundam* saga pushes the entire giant robot subgenre further into the future.

In *Key the Metal Idol* (1994), the robot Tokiko Mima, also known as Key, has lived with humans since she was created by Dr. Mima. When Dr. Mima dies, he leaves a message for Key: she must somehow get thirty thousand people to feel strong emotions for her. If she's able to do this, then she will become "fully" human. The new twist in *Key* is that the robot is trying to become human. Key isn't battling other mecha in giant space wars. Key is just trying to have emotions.

In 1995–2002, *Ghost in the Shell* appeared in the anime world. This series marked another major breakthrough in anime, and while it features cyborgs and cybernetically enhanced humans, it's not typically classified as a mecha anime. We focus more on *Ghost in the Shell* in chapter 3, but for now, just keep in mind that *Ghost* gave us hacked computers, hacked brains, brain-computer interfaces, and other *Neuromancer*-type scenarios. We talk about *Ghost* a bit below, particularly in the section on man-machine interfaces and prosthetics, because it features characters such as Kusanagi Motoko, who has a full cyborg body but a flesh brain, and Batou, who is part cyborg and part flesh.

Along with giant robots, the mid-1990s gave us a lot of anime that focus on man-machine interfaces. Along with the power-house *Ghost in the Shell*, 1995 gave us shows such as *Genocyber*, in which a mad scientist merges the broken body of one daughter with the broken brain of another, thus creating a psychic-cybernetic monster called Genocyber. Earth's cities have been destroyed, everything's in flames, there are few human survivors. Genocyber knows that she is the cause of all that's gone wrong on Earth, and so she goes into a deep sleep, hiding beneath Ark De Grande, a city of violence, corruption, and mayhem. So again, we have a cyber-being who has emotions. Beneath the city, a religious group spurs rebellion and worships Genocyber as a god.

Escaflowne in 1996 aired twenty-six episodes and included touches of mecha, though for the most part, this anime was a romantic fantasy. Heroine Hitomi Kanzaki is transported to Gaea, a mysterious world that thinks of Earth as the Mystic Moon. (We'll talk more about *Escaflowne* in our chapter about parallel universes.) Along with medieval knights and Hitomi's psychic powers, *Escaflowne* incorporates mecha battle suits called Guymelefs. The knights wear them during battle, and one of the Guymelefs is named Escaflowne. In terms of mecha, there's not much new here.

Other major anime involving some mecha include 1991's *Bubblegum Crisis* and *Bubblegum Crash* and 1998's *Bubblegum Crisis*

2040. The main thrust of these major shows, however, is artificial intelligence, which we discuss later in this book. In these shows, artificial humanoid robots called Boomers evolve; they are used by humans as slave labor. Some Boomers, the BU-335 Sexaroids in particular, are used for slave sex. A vigilante force called the Knight Sabers pilot mecha suits to battle Boomers who go crazy and try to revolt against their human masters.

Bubblegum adds a new twist to the robot-mecha subgenre in that it introduces the idea of using robots for slave labor and sex. Its theme of artificial life asks the now old question: What does it mean to be human if you evolved artificially?

A groundbreaking anime appeared in 1996 in the form of *Neon Genesis Evangelion.* In 2015, humans are pitted against each other in war, with most of Earth destroyed by what appears to be a meteorite strike on Antarctica that results in direct devastation as well as the melting of the polar ice caps. Now, people are living in subterranean cities. Mysterious beings called Angels attack, and humankind's only hope for survival is the tactics of the teenage-piloted Evangelions, which are gigantic biomechanical humanoid mechas with man-machine neural interfaces to their young pilots. Shinji is the terrified boy who must operate the Evangelion that can defeat the Angels. The left arm of the Evangelion regenerates itself, a mecha tactic we saw in 1994's *Mobile Suit Fighter G Gundam. Evangelion* was revolutionary mainly because it offered an intricate plot, elaborate animations, and heavy (and we mean *heavy*) emotions.

Then, in 1998, mecha anime appeared in its older form in *Gasaraki,* in which bipedal combat machines are used in war. However, these giant robots aren't on stage constantly—they're just clashing to add stage presence. The story is intricate, and the shows are filled with plenty of technobabble.

Also in 1998 appeared two anime series briefly mentioned earlier in this chapter: *Getter Robo* and *Shin Getter Robo.* In *Getter Robo,* the Dinosaur Kingdom sends mechanical dinosaurs from their subterranean haunts up to the surface of Earth. The objective is to obliterate all humans. A mechanical dinosaur destroys the prototype Getter Robo, so the Saotome Research Institute sends out the "real" Getter Robo. Then, in *Shin Getter Robo,* pilot Ryoma Nagare is jailed for supposedly killing Dr. Saotome, the creator of the Getter Robo. But Saotome comes back from the dead and tries to destroy the world using his latest invention, called Shin Dragon. Nagare must use Getter Robo to battle Saotome and his Shin Dragon. Nearly 99 percent of all life on Earth is destroyed during the battles. Even after a nuclear blast, even after thirteen years of destruction, there are pockets of humankind left, still battling Saotome's evil creations. On the side of humanity is Shin Getter, who emerges form the nuclear debris piloted by Go, an artificial human. Nothing particularly new here was added to the mecha anime subgenre, unless you count the piloting of the mecha by an artificial human. Nonetheless, they're good shows.

We should also mention *Big O* and *Big O II,* circa 1999, in which no one in Paradigm City has any memory of what happened forty years ago or more. Roger Smith pilots a giant robot called Big O, and he also has an android called R. Dorothy Wayneright. With these two figures, and his butler-mechanic Norman Burg, Smith tries to protect Paradigm City from the people who are slowly regaining their memories and rebuilding whatever atrocities led to monsters in the past. Again, there's nothing dramatic here in terms of robotic science that we haven't seen in other anime, but the *Big O* series is famous enough in fan circles that it warrants note.

In *Betterman,* which appeared in 1999, we find another subterranean world, called Bottomworld, where people are living in bleak surroundings. After hundreds of people die during an "accident," a teenage boy runs endlessly through the darkness until he comes across a beautiful young girl with long pink hair. She's strapped to a chair and jacked into equipment, an advanced military system of some kind. She cannot be unleashed from the equipment, she says; and we later learn that this has something to do with neurology and dopamine levels. Neuro-noids are mentioned by scientists, as are synapse attacks and other neurological buzzword phrases. Undercover agents are using Neuro-noids to battle the deadly Algernon virus. So once again, the mecha are hooked up to teenagers using a neural conduit of some kind.

Also in 1999, the anime *Now and Then, Here and There* featured giant robotic snakes. Not quite mecha in the traditional sense, though the series also included giant, standard robots that appear vaguely reminiscent of R2-D2s. The main focus of *Now and Then, Here and There* was the time warps created by giant machines. (Everything in this show is giant!)

In 2001, a landmark anime aired. It was known as *Metropolis* and soon became a classic. Based on the comic by Osamu Tezuka, the screenplay was written by Japanese anime legend Katsuhiro Otomo (who also wrote *Akira*). *Metropolis* features another subterranean *Blade Runner*–type world. In this world, Duke Red, the leader, is going to unveil his new robot creation, Tima. Duke's son, Rock, hates all robots, however, and tries to destroy Tima. Tima runs away into the subterranean mazes.

In *Metropolis,* humans use robots for labor, much as in earlier anime. Here, the robots and humans aren't getting along very well. In the meantime, a private investigator who is central to the story obtains a police robot from "robot storage" and is told that his robot need only be refueled once every five years. The human who supplies the robot bemoans the fact that, soon, robots will take all human jobs. The police robot has a name: it is Model 803-D-RP-DM-497-3-C. The robot explains that he's not allowed to have a human name because humans would feel threatened. The detective, Shunsaku Ban, calls the robot Pero. So right away, we know that we're watching an anime that attempts to answer questions such as: What defines humanity? How are humans different from artificially intelligent robots? What does it mean to be human?

The robots are treated like worthless hunks of metal. Humans throw them into garbage gyros, huge machines used to collect disobedient robots and grind them up; this is the penalty for venturing beyond authorized zones for robots. Humans use the robots to fight fires, to rescue people, to collect trash, and to operate as basic medics. There are dog robots, clown robots, servant butler robots. Eventually, magnetic radiation sweeps Metropolis (i.e., science has gone haywire), robots start short-circuiting and exploding, and cops start shooting at the robots (if we want to turn off our computers, that's what we do: we shoot them with guns). People are demanding antirobot laws.

Eventually, Tima the robot ends up ruling the world. She is desperate to know if she's human. After all, she has emotions and feels love. But no, she's told that she's only a robot, albeit a remarkable robot. Her emotions will dissolve when she assumes the throne, and in time, she will become a weapon of war. If *Metropolis* is saying anything about robots, it's that they have the potential to be far more humane than humans; it is also saying that human leaders are heartless warmongers.

As the world is inundated by biological warfare, killing all flesh life, Tima weeps that she's not just a robot, she's a humanoid; then, she sits upon her throne and merges her mind with the vast worldwide data network. Because of Tima's quick fall into warmonger cruelty and because of her robotic control of the worldwide data networks, within 17 hours and 27 minutes, all humans will be dead due to biological warfare.

After a long battle with Ken Ichi, whom she had loved when

she was a robot, Tima turns into a strange blob creature of cables, goo, and electricity. And as if all this weren't weird enough, *Metropolis* ends with a blast of the song *I Can't Stop Loving You.* And then the world blows up. This is not exactly a lighthearted cartoon show. It's anime in its finest form.

Also in 2001, *Mahoromatic* featured the android Mahoro, who wants to live her last year as a human. The secret agency Vesper is using super-strong battle androids to fight alien invaders, and Mahoro is the most powerful battle droid in Vesper's horde. But her operating time is dwindling, and so, to be human, she chooses to live her last year as a maid for the high school student Suguru. Like *Metropolis,* though in a less powerful way, *Mahoromatic* delves into questions about what it means to be human and what it means to be an android. And in a slightly new twist, we have a battle mecha who takes off her armor to become a maid.

While it may seem to anime newcomers that we're describing the bulk of the different anime series that have appeared, in actuality, we're describing only a small percentage of them. It would take many volumes to cover all the mecha anime shows that have ever aired. Instead, we're trying to touch on what we think are some of the high points in mecha and robotic anime, series that changed the subgenre and pushed it forward a little into the future.

So with that in mind, we move to 2002's *RahXephon.* We considered omitting this series from the chapter because it seemed so similar to many other shows, but decided to include it due to its tremendous popularity. In this series, Tokyo has been overthrown (a common anime theme), and what little is left of the human race is battling the Mu and their Dolem. RahXephon is a humanoid weapon that hatched from an egg beneath the wreckage of Tokyo. RahXephon looks like a 164-foot-tall god, and has superpowers and wings. It rotates light around its head, and then uses that light to zap enemies. Basically, RahXephon is a giant battle robot with angel wings and a halo who has hatched from an egg. Could the new twist here be a form of biotechnology, perhaps, or nanotechnology?

In 2003, *Texhnolyze* featured yet another bleak metropolis buried beneath the ground. As is often the case in anime, the miserable subterranean city is ruled by gangs and subject to constant revolution. In *Texhnolyze*, those in power are the ones strong enough to remove the limbs from their enemies. Cybernetic replacements are attached to people who have lost their limbs, and their replacements are devised using a mysterious technology known as Texhnolyze, which attaches the central nervous system to the prosthetic devices. This idea is based on real technology, which we'll describe later in this chapter.

We've talked about 1979's *Mobile Suit Gundam,* 1994's *Mobile Fighter Gundam,* and 1995–96's *Mobile Suit Gundam Wing.* In 2002–2003, *Mobile Suit Gundam SEED* aired. Thanks to genetic engineering, the world is populated with a new kind of human known as Coordinators; they live in space colonies. The old-fashioned, ordinary humans are known as Naturals. True to

Gundam form, war breaks out between the Coordinators in space and the people left on Earth. The Earthlings create five new Gundam mobile suits—in secret, of course. But the Coordinators raid the secret lab and steal four of the Gundam suits.

There are even more *Gundam* series, actually, such as 2004's *Mobile Suit Gundam SEED DESTINY,* in which three new prototype Gundams are stolen from a secret plant. But for now, it's enough to know that *Mobile Suit Gundam SEED* delved into the subject of genetic engineering; the mecha themselves didn't evolve significantly from earlier shows in the Gundam saga.

So where does all of this lead us?

We notice certain themes recurring in mecha anime, including:

- Exoskeletons (powered armor that people wear)
- Remotely controlled and piloted robots
- Robots that think they're human
- Man-machine interfaces and cybernetic limbs, also known as prosthetic devices

Let's look at each theme briefly in terms of real science.

Exoskeletons

We define exoskeletons as powered armor that people wear. A huge number of the mecha anime, as we've discussed extensively in this chapter, feature suits that operate as powered armor, either by humans wearing the suits or by robots wearing them. In fact, this sort of powered armor exists today.

In real life, a human exoskeleton suit consists of a robotic-type device that can be strapped on or attached directly to the human body. The device adds muscle power for heavy lifting, long-range running, and walking. It also enables the user to wear heavy armor without being affected by the weight. Not only are exoskeletons popular in anime, they've been common in Marvel Comics for decades, as the favorite uniform of many mercenaries working for outlaw political groups such as A.I.M. and H.Y.D.R.A. Exoskeletons played a major role in the third Matrix film, *Revolutions,* and one helped save the day for Ripley in *Aliens.* After decades of being promoted by pop culture, comic books, and cartoons, exoskeletons are now on the verge of becoming reality. At least, that is, if the U.S. government has anything to say about it.

In January 2001, DARPA (the U.S. Defense Advanced Research Projects Agency) awarded approximately $50 million in contracts to laboratories and experimental groups to develop technology aimed at building an exoskeleton suit for ground troops. Dr. Ephrahim Garcia, coordinator of the project, said that the goals of the program are "formidable" and that "there is a huge challenge here." Dr. Garcia made it clear that the exoskeleton suit had to be something that soldiers could wear and use without thinking, and not something controlled by switches.[1]

The exoskeleton would have to be able to perform specific tasks spelled out by DARPA:

1. Increase strength: Troops must be able to carry heavier packs (including body armor), lift heavy objects, and use larger weapons.
2. Increase speed: Troops should be able to march faster over longer distances.
3. Increase leaping ability: Troops would be able to leap extraordinary heights and distances.

The first exoskeleton requirement would enable soldiers to carry large weapons into battle. At present, soldiers carry a backpack that is no more than one-third of their weight, and often much less, into war zones. It's common for soldiers to leave behind any equipment too heavy to carry for long amounts of time. The extra power requirement would also enable the exoskeletons to carry up to ten pounds of extra protective gear for the user, not counting the armor on the exoskeleton itself.

Early work sponsored by DARPA involved pneumatic muscles or deformable magnets to power artificial limbs or suits that soldiers could wear. Pneumatic muscles were first invented in the early 1950s by physicist J. L. McKibben to help polio patients. These muscles were similar to balloons, which, when put under pressure, acted like pneumatic springs. The correct pressure in the balloon was maintained by a gas cartridge that produced carbon dioxide. At the Man-Machine Systems Department at the Delft University of Technology in the Netherlands, scientist Richard van der Linde used pneumatic muscles to construct a walking robot he named BAPS (Biped with Adjustable Pneumatic Springs).[2] In the United States, the SpringWalker system from Applied Motion, Inc., developed for the exoskeleton research project, propelled its user at speeds greater than fifteen miles per hour.

Another goal for the exoskeletons would be that they require no refueling for at least twenty-four hours, and that they move silently. The exoskeletons would also include a sensor web, expanding the user's field of vision; and use thermal cameras to relay information about the battlefield to the wearer. Groups of soldiers wearing exoskeletons would be connected by global satellite positioning systems, enabling them to track each other in any situation.[3]

Are these goals unrealistic? The officials at DARPA and the scientists already working on test projects don't think so. Back in 1965, General Electric Research and Development Center, working with the U.S. military, developed an exoskeleton powered by hydraulics and electricity they called Hardiman, which made lifting 250 pounds feel like lifting 10 pounds. Unfortunately, the inventors of the robot, which weighed several tons, could get only one arm of the machine to work at a time.[4]

Recent results have been more encouraging. Researchers at Oak Ridge National Laboratory have invented a machine that can amplify hand motions to move heavy objects with ease and precision. This lifter can raise a thousand-pound bomb as easily as a can of cola.[5]

Scientists at the University of California, Berkeley's Human Engineering Laboratory have constructed a highly advanced motorized exoskeleton to help disabled people walk. The exoskeleton weighs as much as a normal man and is powered by a chainsaw engine. However, when attached to a researcher's back and legs, it supports him as he walks, with the weight of the machinery completely unnoticed.[6]

Exoskeletons are coming—perhaps sooner than anyone realizes. The walking device described in the previous paragraph is not far from being used by disabled people. Long-term plans call for complete human exoskeletons by 2010. The cost per unit is projected to be about the same cost as a motorcycle. The face of warfare is about to change—in real life—toward what we see in mecha anime.

Remotely Controlled and Piloted Robots

In addition to mecha mobile suits used for battle, anime features plenty of remotely controlled robots, many with human pilots. How close to reality are these scenarios? Do we have robots today that are remotely controlled?

Of course we do.

In reality circa 2005, humankind has sent robots into the

electromagnetic fields of Jupiter; and Pioneers, Pathfinders, Mariners, Vikings, and Voyagers have probed, retrieved samples, snapped and transmitted images, and analyzed data from all over the solar system. We have been on the moon, and, indirectly via probes, on many other worlds beyond Earth. Remote control mechanisms are very common with robots.

After the terrorist attack on the World Trade Center on September 11, 2001, "marsupial" robots, which carry smaller robots inside them to explore tight spaces, crawled through the wreckage of the twin towers searching for survivors. Dozens of robots were used, armed with bright lights, and heat and motion detectors. Some of the machines were remotely controlled, while others were connected to the users by cables. The robots rode on Caterpillar tracks and were powerful enough to push pieces of concrete out of their way.[7]

How Humans and Artificially Intelligent Robots Differ

While we cover this subject in depth in chapter 3, it's worth mentioning here that by definition, artificial intelligence (AI) has to do with the ability of computers to think independently. Of course, the concept revolves around the basic question of how we define intelligence. And that's also the focus in anime series that question why robots can't be humans and therefore what humans essentially *are.* Prime examples are *Neon Genesis Evangelion, Key the Metal Idol,* and, of course, *Metropolis.* Machine intelligence has always been a compromise between what we understand about our own thought processes and what we can program a machine to do. When the machine starts learning on its own, as human babies and children do (and some grown-ups), we define it as artificially intelligent. It is the ability to learn, to adapt to different environments, and to experience emotions, such as love and greed, that define the core nature of human intelligence. In *Metropolis,* while humans destroy the entire world and all life on it, robots have the capacity to experience positive emotions, such as love, kindness, and the appreciation of beauty. Perhaps, in this case, the robots are more human than the humans themselves? Again, we touch on this subject here because the concept of AI is integral to robotics in mecha anime. But the concept of AI in anime is so huge—from mecha anime to nonmecha shows such as *Astro Boy* and *Roujin Z*—that we devote an entire chapter to the subject.

Man-Machine Interfaces and Prosthetics in Real Life

As mentioned above, 2003's *Texhnolyze* used prosthetic limbs as a key plot device. People rose to power by destroying the biological limbs of others; and then those without arms, for example, got cybernetic, or prosthetic, replacements. *Ghost in the Shell* also made extensive use of cybernetically enhanced humans. In this anime, Kusanagi Motoko has a full cyborg body with a flesh brain—to name just one example.

In reality, prosthetic limbs are artificial replacements of flesh-and-blood limbs, and they are used by many real people.

Peg legs are the simplest type of prostheses; they have no electronic components. Another simple type of artificial appendage is an arm that ends with pincers rather than a hand. This simple limb is attached to whatever is left of the patient's real arm. It is also attached to a harness that is strapped around the patient's shoulders. When the patient moves his or her shoulder, the harness moves, pulling cables that open and close the hooks.

However, far more sophisticated devices do exist. Dynamic prostheses contain electronic components and are based on myoelectric properties. A myoelectric prosthesis contains sensors that respond to the electricity created by the movement of flesh-and-blood muscles. When a patient tenses his or her muscles—say, in the upper arm—the sensors in the prosthetic portion of the arm detect the myoelectric transmission and send the corresponding signals to the artificial hand. Run by batteries, the hand opens or closes. Some prosthetic limbs even have sensors that detect temperature. These devices send hot and cold information to electrodes in the skin, enabling a patient to "feel" with the prosthetic limbs.

Today's advances include artificial feet that cushion the body on the ground as if they were real, and feet with electronic components that enable patients to balance their weight more evenly. For example, the Elation Flex-Foot from a company called Össur contains "flex-foot technology" along with adjustable heel heights. The Elation Flex-Foot automatically adjusts its mechanical pieces— known as foot blades and rocker plates—based on the amount of weight placed upon it. If a patient is heavier than average, if he or she shifts his or her weight from one foot to the other, or if he or she leans heavily in one direction, the foot blade presses more strongly against the rocker plate, thus changing the cushioning or impact of the foot against the ground. According to Össur, "A narrow, anatomically correct foot cover with a sandal toe contour is bonded to the foot, making it suitable for dress shoes, sandals, cowboy boots, and other types of footwear. Elation is easy to cosmetically finish and the foot is ideal for amputees of low and moderate impact levels weighing up to 220 pounds."[8]

For amputees who have lost legs at the hip level, modern medicine provides artificial hip joints made of laminated plastic or a thermoplastic.

Prosthetic devices are commonly made from carbon fibers, titanium, and polypropylenes, which are flexible plastics. Prostheses can also be constructed of a bulletproof material called Kevlar. To make limbs really strong, a prosthetic can be made with a layer of carbon, a layer of Kevlar, and another layer of carbon.

According to *Medical Device & Diagnostic Industry* magazine,[9] much research is going into creating materials that emulate human muscles. For example, a full-size plastic skeleton named Mr. Boney roams around the University of New Mexico Artificial Muscle Research Institute. Mr. Boney's microprocessor-controlled heart pumps a chemical fluid through his body, and this fluid is what actuates his artificial muscles.

Israeli scientists discovered in the 1940s that polymer fiber gels shrink in acid solutions. They also expand when a base is added to the acid solutions. Apparently, these properties are similar to those of biological muscles. Another way of making "robotic muscles" contract and swell is to expose them to electrical currents.

Modern research focuses on making artificial muscles respond more quickly and more significantly to chemical and electrical stimulation. In other words, researchers are trying to get artificial muscles to lift more weight and to do it more quickly.

Dr. Qiming Zhang, professor of electrical engineering at the Pennsylvania State University Materials Research Institute, bombards copolymer material with electrons to make it more flexible.[10] As voltage increases, the copolymer material becomes increasingly capable of movement—in fact, up to forty times more movement than other materials used in prosthetics.[11]

It takes approximately 100 milliseconds for human muscles to respond to transmissions from the brain. Using new materials and techniques, modern prosthetics can move at near-human speeds. Unfortunately, the strength of these prosthetics remains limited. This issue is being addressed by Mohsen Shahinpoor of the University of New Mexico, who has developed artificial muscles made from thousands of strands of polyacrylonitrile. These muscles are twice as strong as human muscles.

By combining artificial intelligence, robotics, sensors, micromachinery, distributed processing, and other technologies, scientists will create a wide variety of smart materials and devices over the next couple of decades.[12]

First, let's define the term *smart materials*. According to a company that specializes in creating them, smart materials are "any material that shows some form of response (often physical) such as mechanical deformation, movement, optical illumination, heat generation, contraction, and expansion in presence of a given stimulus, such as electricity, heat, light, chemicals, pressure, mechanical deformation, exposure to other chemicals or elements. The response may be useful in converting the applied energy into a desired motion or action."[13]

Soon, smart materials will be in everything from computers to concrete bridges. According to *Scientific American*, "Forget dumb old bricks and mortar: engineers are designing future devices from exotic materials that incorporate chemical switches or mechanical sensors to improve their performance. These 'smart materials' are just starting to emerge from the laboratory, but soon you can expect to find them in everything from laptop computers to concrete bridges. Philip Troyk of the Illinois Institute of Technology has constructed wireless sensors no larger than a Rice Krispie. Implanted in a patient's muscle, the devices could relay information on local nerve activity via radio to an external computer. The devices could also receive power through magnetic induction and send out mild shocks that stimulate the muscle into action."[14]

Sandia National Laboratories in Albuquerque, New Mexico, is currently conducting research about embedding these smart materials and devices in walls, doors, and other building structures. Sandia's smart materials will "sense disturbances, process the information and through commands to actuators, accomplish some beneficial reaction such as vibration control." Their work includes flexible robotics, photo-lithography (the manufacture of smaller microelectronic circuits), biomechanical and biomedical (artificial muscles, drug delivery systems) direction, and process control of solar reflectors and aerodynamic surfaces.[15]

When we start thinking about the bridges between biological systems and electronics, we couple thoughts of smart devices and materials with the fields of biotechnology and nanotechnology.

We think of *biotechnology* as the systems that tie biology to technology. For example, an implant that regulates blood chemistry is a biotech device.

Nanotechnology, on the other hand, refers to microscopic systems; *nano* itself means a billionth; thus, a nanometer, the size used to measure these microscopic systems, is one billionth of a meter. Something created with nanotechnology need not be fused with biological systems; it need not exist in our bodies, for example. Someday, we'll have nanotech systems embedded everywhere: microscopic, interconnected, and widely distributed networked systems that exist in our walls, shoes, hats, pillows, and transportation vehicles, as well as in our very flesh.

In terms of biotechnology, neurotrophic electrodes are already in use. Says futurist Michael Zey, "Other diseases and disorders are being treated with neural implants in what is being called 'deep brain simulation' therapies. Doctors have achieved some success in using such implants to reduce tremors associated with cerebral palsy, multiple sclerosis, and other tremor-causing diseases. They are doing this by implanting electrodes in a section of the brain called the ventral lateral thalamus."[16]

A paralyzed man with an implanted neurotrophic electrode is now communicating with a computer system. The electrode, devised by Emory University Hospital scientists, is coated with chemicals that stimulate connections between the implant, the surrounding nerve tissue, and the man's brain. Electrical signals run through the connections, and the electrode transmits them to a receiver on the surface of the man's scalp. He requires no wires running from his scalp beneath his skin. Remember that this man is paralyzed—that is, he cannot physically move. However, using the neurotrophic electrode, he is able to transmit signals from his brain to a computer. He moves the cursor on the screen, selecting letters to spell words, and it is hoped that he'll soon be sending email.[17]

The *New York Times* reported that, in 1996, scientists received FDA approval to create brain-computer interfaces in almost-dead patients. Again, ideal patients were those without any motor control and suffering from brain-stem damage—similar to the paralyzed man just described. The first operation took place in 1998. By imagining he could move his paralyzed left hand, the first patient triggered an increase in his brain's electrical impulses, and these impulses were transmitted to a receiver on his pillow. The receiver translated the analog brain signals into digital computer signals, and passed the digital results to a computer. Using this method, the patient could move a cursor on the computer screen.[18]

As for nanotechnology, early forms of devices using it, and their applications, may be available soon. However, it seems unlikely that in the imminent future, we will have nanotech machines coursing through our veins, cleansing us of fat—or nanotech machines in our brains, serving as cyberpunk computers, possibly downloading our minds onto Crays or uploading the encyclopedia of the world into our skulls. Some experts predict that we're already on the cusp of nanotechnology, but that may be due to slight differences in how we define the term.

James D. Plummer, professor of electrical engineering at Stanford University, notes, "Perhaps the broadest definition of a 'nanostructure' is something which has a physical dimension smaller than 0.1 micron, or 100 nanometers (billionths of a meter). . . . Based on current rates of development, people have projected that around the year 2005 companies will be manufacturing in high-volume integrated circuits that have dimensions around 0.1 micron. . . . So if size alone defines nanotechnology, then every one of us is seeing practical benefits of it today."[19]

However, Plummer also points out that nanotechnology usually connotes nano-sized *machines*. K. Eric Drexler, the author of the groundbreaking *Engines of Creation: The Coming Era of Nanotechnology*, defines nanotechnology to include: "molecular manufacturing, that is, products can be assembled on the nanometer scale with extreme precision allowing the rearrangement of individual atoms and molecules; materials with novel and/or adaptable properties, controllable by molecular manufacturing; miniaturization of electronic and mechanical parts down to the atomic scale, leading to nanomachines, whose compactness and efficiency could even outperform the cellular systems."[20] Plummer agrees, and further states that it will be at least twenty-five years before we have nanotech machines cleaning fat from our arteries.[21] The *New York Times* predicts that we'll have to wait about thirty years.[22]

Nanotechnology research is booming. On April 27, 2001, *Wired* magazine reported, "The quest for nanometer-scale computing is now a quantum leap closer to reality. In Friday's issue of the journal *Science*, physicists from IBM's Thomas J. Watson Research Center announce their fabrication of the world's first array of transistors made from carbon nanotubes."[23]

There's a reason why carbon nanotubes are so exciting to today's scientists. Early computers used switches that were actually vacuum tubes—large glass tubes in which electric current passed freely between metal wires. A "binary on" was when electrons were flowing in the tube. A "binary off" was when they were not. Later, semiconductor transistors took over the work of the vacuum tube. As a result, our computers became smaller and much more powerful. Today, experts believe that carbon nanotubes of rolled-up graphite may replace transistors. These nanotubes measure only a few nanometers in diameter.[24]

Other areas of nanotech-related research are also pushing forward at a rapid pace. In November 2000, *Wired* reported that major work was occurring in the field of "nanotechnology—also known as bio-micro-electromechanical systems, or bioMEMS— as a means to deliver drugs, supplements, and therapies to specific sites in the body or to draw out a dosage over weeks, months, or years."[25] BioMEMS, as its name implies, combines biology and genetics with advances in computer and electronics technologies. For example, researchers are investigating techniques that combine robotic heart surgery and microchip technologies. Dr. Robert Michler, director of research and the chief of cardiothoracic surgery at the Medical Center at Ohio State University, explains that his team coats microchips with chemicals such as insulin, gene therapies, and heart medicines. Human clinical trials will begin in five years, and his team is already creating chips in hopes of using robots to insert them into animal hearts. As Professor Albert Pisano, director of the Electronics Research Laboratory at the University of California, Berkeley, states, "It's already science fact, not science fiction."[26]

3. Artificial Intelligence

An Overview of AI

You probably remember from chapter 2 that as far back as 1952, Tetsuwan Atomu was a "little boy" robot in whom beat the heart of his inventor's son. Atomu was a humane robot. He had emotions, though he didn't have artificial intelligence. He was more like the tin man in *The Wizard of Oz*, who wanted a heart.

In 1988, *Mobile Police Patlabor* featured artificially intelligent robots used as tools, police machines, and exploration vehicles. But it wasn't until 1995's *Neon Genesis Evangelion* that anime truly posed questions about whether artificially intelligent robots can be considered "alive" or whether they are merely machines. The robots in *Evangelion* are beings who evolved from Adam, the original Angel; these robots prevent the world from being destroyed by other Angels. People pilot the robots via manmachine interfaces: that is, between the human brain and nervous system and the robot's computer circuitry, as described in chapter 2.

In *Key the Metal Idol* (1994), the robot Tokiko Mima, known as Key, can become "fully" human if she is able to get thirty thousand people to feel strong emotions for her.

Then the classic *Ghost in the Shell* (1995–2002) featured hacked computers, hacked brains, and brain-computer interfaces. And as noted in chapter 2, there are many other examples of anime that rely on man-machine interfaces and artificially intelligent robots who long to be human as main plot devices: *Genocyber, Bubblegum Crisis, Bubblegum Crash, Bubblegum Crisis 2040, Mahoromatic,* and of course, *Metropolis.*

In this section, we talk about a few other anime series that explored the notion of artificially intelligent robots: *Astro Boy, Chobits,* and *Roujin Z.* Then we dive into the meat of this section: What is artificial intelligence, and how does it differ from human intelligence? Are artificially intelligent robots humans or mere machines? And finally, what will it mean to be human when people have slowly but surely integrated thinking robots into every aspect of life?

The Shows

We begin with *Astro Boy,* who is the offshoot of Tetsuwan Atomu, the robot boy with a human heart. In 2004, Astro Boy was inducted into Carnegie Mellon University's Robot Hall of Fame. He shared this honor with such notable fictional robots as *Star Wars'* C-3PO (hey, what about R2-D2, our personal favorite?) and 1956's Robby the Robot, who starred in *Forbidden Planet*. According to Carnegie Mellon, "The Robot Hall of Fame recognizes excellence in robotics technology worldwide and honors the fictional and real robots that have inspired and made breakthrough accomplishments in robotics."[27] Only five robots were inducted, which gives you some idea as to how significant science fiction and anime robots are in today's world.

So what's the story behind Astro Boy, anyway?

According to the series, which takes place in approximately the year 2000 (which seemed like the distant future when *Astro Boy* was created), robot technology is extremely advanced and robot workers are everywhere around the world. There are robot nurses, firefighters, and factory workers.

The head of the Ministry of Science, Dr. Boyton, is obsessed with creating a robot who has a soul and human emotions. His son, Toby, suggests that Boyton create a "boy" robot, so that's what the doctor does.

Because Boyton ditches his personal life to focus exclusively on his job, Toby runs away from home and is killed in a car accident. Boyton completes his "boy" robot by giving him a soul very much like his own son's soul. Astro Boy leaps into life where Toby left off: he calls Boyton and his wife Mom and Dad; he plays with Toby's dog, Jump; and he treats Toby's sister, Uran, as his own. Astro Boy attends school with human children, makes friends, and even gets into trouble as if he were a real human boy. Astro Boy brings up the intriguing notion of artificial intelligence inside humanoid bodies. Is this possible? We'll find out later in this chapter when we talk about the science.

Chobits differs from *Astro Boy* in that it focuses on artificially intelligent robots who function as servants, companions, and, most significantly, sexy girlfriends. The main character is nineteen-year-old Hideki, who finds Chi, a Persocom humanoid robot companion, in a trash heap. Of course, Hideki has never had much luck with girls in the past. He doesn't know what to do with the sexy, beautiful Chi, who's every boy's dream. She also happens to be a computer, and Hideki's never been very adept with them, either. Luckily for Hideki, Chi falls for him and adores him as her one true love. As Hideki teaches Chi how to do things, he begins to realize that she's a lot smarter than he initially thought. In fact, Chi might be a very advanced form of artificial intelligence known as a Chobit.

Other people in *Chobits* have Persocoms, or know somebody who does. For example, female teacher Takako Shimizu's husband becomes obsessed with his adorable Persocom, ignoring his wife. She has to find her own comfort elsewhere. Hideki's classmate, Shimbo Hiroshi, is obsessed with his Persocom, as well.

Another Persocom named Yuzuki is supposedly the most advanced Persocom ever built. But Yuzuki isn't sentient, according to the series, because she can't learn beyond her initial programming. Chi, on the other hand, can learn beyond her initial programming, and thus is sentient, or artificially intelligent. Although Chi possesses artificial intelligence, she doesn't do a lot of things that most computers do: she doesn't connect to the

Internet, she doesn't have word processing programs, she doesn't communicate with other Persocoms.

As Hideki and Chi fall in love, someone kidnaps her. The kidnapper, or computer-napper, is possibly a former owner who is also in love with her. Or perhaps she retains secrets about the former owner, dangerous secrets that the former owner wants to hide forever. Hideki wonders now, more than ever, whether an artificial intelligence is truly human or just a machine. He feels driven to save Chi from harm, as if she were a human lover. He wonders if Chi's memories are stored on a hard drive. If so, it's possible that her memories can be deleted, which would mean that her memories aren't really her own; if so, how can she be a person? Furthermore, after someone has been in love with a perfect humanoid Persocom—brilliant, beautiful, loving, giving in all ways—how can he or she ever love a mere human again? Does the Persocom have a soul? What is a soul? These are all basic questions that come up when we ponder the differences between humans and artificially intelligent machines.

Another anime series, called *Roujin Z*, gave us artificially intelligent computers that act as caretakers for the elderly. In this unusual show, the number of elderly people in Japan is rising quickly, and to take care of their needs, the government creates caretaker machines. Student nurse Haruko has a patient, Mr. Takazawa, who is one of the subjects of the government's experiments in automated elderly care. Mr. Takazawa's bed happens to be artificially intelligent. It bathes the senior citizen, talks to him,

entertains him, feeds him, and basically takes care of his every need by linking directly to his brain. And of course, it has an Internet hookup. After awhile, as Takazawa attempts to escape from the bed with Haruko's help, the bed starts thinking that it's the old man's dead wife. And the wife, of course, doesn't want her husband escaping from her. Haruko discovers that the bed has a biochip, which is why it thinks it's Takazawa's wife.

We talk extensively about *Ghost in the Shell* elsewhere in this book, but it's also a series that explores what it means to be human versus a machine, what evolution means, what life itself means. Motoko sees herself everywhere: other humanoids look identical to her, yet she has her own thoughts and ideas, so she prefers to think of herself as a unique individual, a human. She also believes that she has a soul. If an artificial intelligence generates its own soul, is the machine human or mere machine? That is, do you have to be born with a soul, or can you create your own? As with *Chobits*, we're confronted with the question: Just what is a soul?

The Science

Just what is artificial intelligence? How similar are the human brain and a computer? Can a computer use the brain for data storage? What does it mean to be human as opposed to artificially intelligent?

As mentioned in chapter 2, AI has to do with the ability of computers to think independently, and the concept revolves around the basic question of how we define intelligence.[28] Norbert Wiener, one of the greatest scientists of this century, was among the first to note the similarities between human thought and machine operation in the science of cybernetics that he helped found. Cybernetics takes its name from the Greek word for "helmsman." Typically, a helmsman steers his ship in a fixed direction: toward a star or a point on land, or along a given compass heading. Whatever waves or wind throw the ship off this heading, the helmsman brings it back on course. This process, in which deviations result in corrections back to a set point, is called negative feedback. (The opposite, positive feedback, occurs when deviations from a set point result in further deviations. The nuclear arms race is the classic example.) A common example of the use of negative feedback is a thermostat. It measures a room's temperature, then turns the heat on or off to keep the room at a desired temperature. Wiener theorized that all intelligent behavior could be traced to feedback mechanisms. Since feedback processes could be expressed as algorithms, this meant that theoretically, intelligence could be built into a machine.

This simple way of looking at human logic and applying it to machines provided a foundation for computer science theory. Early artificial intelligence attempted to reduce our thought processes to purely logical steps and then encode the steps for use by a computer. A computer functions at its lowest level by switching between two states: binary one for true, and zero for false. Circuits are made from combinations of ones and zeros. This fact about circuits carried some inherent limitations: it meant that computers could calculate only through long chains of yes-no, true-false statements of the form "If A is true, go to step B; if A is false, go to step C." Statements had to be entirely true or entirely false. A statement that was 60 percent true was vastly more difficult to deal with. (When Lotfi Zadeh began introducing partially true statements into computer science in the

1970s and 1980s—for example, "The sky is cloudy"—many logicians argued that this was not allowable. The field of logic that deals with partially true statements is called fuzzy logic.) Ambiguity, error, and partial information were also problematic. Computers, whose original function, after all, was to compute, were much better equipped to deal with the clean, well-lighted world of mathematical calculation than with the much messier real world. It took some years before computer scientists grasped just how wide the chasm is between these worlds. Moreover, binary logic was best suited to manipulating symbols, which could always be represented as strings of ones and zeros. Geometric and spatial problems were much more difficult. And cases where a symbol could have more than one meaning provoked frequent errors.

Based on yes-no, if-then, true-false statements, the older school of AI is what we call the top-down approach—the heuristic if-then method of applying intelligence to computers. It's very methodical.

A breakthrough decade for top-down AI was the 1950s. Herbert Simon, who later won a Nobel Prize for economics, and Allen Newell, a physicist and mathematician, designed a top-down program called Logic Theorist. Although the program's outward goal was to produce proofs of logic theorems, its real purpose was to help the researchers figure out how people reach conclusions by making correct guesses.

Logic Theorist was a top-down method because it used

decision trees, making its way down various branches until it arrived at either a correct or an incorrect solution. Using this approach, Logic Theorist created an original proof of a mathematical theorem, and Simon and Newell were so impressed that they tried to list the program as coauthor of a technical paper. Sadly, the AI didn't land its publishing credential. The journal in question rejected the manuscript.

In 1956, Dartmouth College in New Hampshire hosted a conference that launched AI research. It was organized by John McCarthy, who coined the term "artificial intelligence." In addition to McCarthy, Simon, Newell, and Logic Theorist (we must list the first recognized AI program as a conference participant), the attendees included Marvin Minsky, who in 1951, with Dean Edmonds, had built a neural-networking machine from vacuum tubes and B-24 bomber parts. Their machine was called SNARC.

As far back as the 1956 conference, artificial intelligence had two definitions. One was top-down: make decisions in a yes-no, if-then, true-false manner—to deduce what's wrong by elimination. The other was quite different, and was later to be called bottom-up: in addition to yes-no, if-then, true-false thinking, AI should also use induction and many of the subtle nuances of human thought.

The main problem with the top-down approach is that it requires an enormous database to store all the possible yes-no facts a computer would have to consider during deduction. It would take an extremely long time to search that database, and would take an extremely long time to arrive at conclusions. It would have to make its way through the mazes upon mazes of logic circuits. This is not at all the way humans think. An astonishing number of thoughts blaze through the human brain all at the same time. In computer lingo, our brains are massive parallel processors.

What top-down AI brings to the table is a symbolic method of representing some of our thought processes in machines. Put more simply, top-down AI converts known human behaviors and thought patterns into computer symbols and instructions.

Perhaps the greatest boost to the top-down philosophy was the defeat of world chess champion Garry Kasparov by the IBM supercomputer Deep Blue on May 11, 1997. Though not artificially intelligent, Deep Blue used a sophisticated if-then program in a convincing display of machine over man. Chess, however, is a game with a rigid set of rules. Players have no hidden moves or resources, and every piece is either on a square or not, taken or not, moveable in a well-defined way or not. There are no rules governing every situation in the real world, and we almost never have complete information. Humans use common sense, intuition, humor, and a wide range of emotions to arrive at conclusions. Love, passion, greed, anger: how do you code these into if-then statements?

From the very beginning of AI research, there were scientists who questioned the top-down approach. Rather than trying to endow the computer with explicit rules for every conceivable situation, these researchers felt it was more logical to work AI in the other direction—to take a bottom-up approach. That is, figure out how to give a computer a foundation of intrinsic capabilities, then let it learn as a child would, on its own, groping its way through the world, making its own connections and conclusions. After all, the human brain is pretty small and doesn't weigh much, and it is not endowed at birth with a massive database with full archives about all the situations it will ever face.

Top-down AI uses inflexible rules and massive databases to draw conclusions, to "think." Bottom-up AI learns from what it does, devises its own rules, creates its own data and conclusions— it adapts and grows in knowledge based on the network environment in which it lives.

Rodney Brooks, a computer scientist at MIT, is one of bottom-up AI's strongest advocates. He believes that AI requires an intellectual springboard similar to animal evolution; that is, an artificially intelligent creature must first learn to survive and prosper in its environment before it can tackle such things as reasoning, intuition, and common sense. It took billions of years for microbes to evolve into vertebrates. It took hundreds of millions of years to move from early vertebrates to modern birds and mammals. It took only a few hundred thousand years for humans to evolve to their present state. So the argument goes: the foundation took forever, yet the development of human reasoning and abstract thought took a mere flash of time.[29] Therefore, current research emphasizes "survival" skills, such as robotic mobility and vision. Robots must have visual sensors and rudimentary intelligence to avoid obstacles and to lift and sort objects.

Based on the definitions of top-down and bottom-up AI, it makes sense to conclude that most anime robots who are artificially intelligent possess bottom-up AI software. That's true even for Astro Boy: he goes to school with human children and learns; he adapts to changes in his environment.

Now, just how similar is the human brain to a computer? We've already described (see chapter 2) current advances in man-machine interfaces that enable the human brain to control computers. Can we run a computer software program using the human brain as the hardware?

There are some very broad similarities between the brain and the computer:

- Both have outputs
- Both are very complex
- Both have physical components (brain tissue/hardware)
- Both have nonphysical components (mind/software)

The brain and the computer have some obvious things in common. Yet despite their similarities, the two things are very different.

The basic circuitry in computers relies on the on-off true-false popping of micro-switches. Neurons in our brain also have on-off true-false states: excited and inhibited. When the voltage across a membrane rises sharply, the neuron is excited and releases chemicals (neurotransmitters) that latch onto receptors of other neurons. When the voltage drops sharply, the neuron is inhibited. Seems awfully similar to the binary on-off states of the computer, doesn't it?

But if we look more closely at neural processes, we see a huge difference. Neurons actually behave in an analog rather than a digital manner.[30] Events leading to neural excitement build up, as if climbing a hill—this is a feature of analog signals. In addition, ions may cross the cell membrane even if neurotransmitters aren't received, and these ions may excite the neuron anyway. Sometimes, a neuron oscillates between intense and mild excitement levels without any outside stimulation. The more a neuron excites itself, the more prone it will be to outside stimulation.

There are approximately fifty neuron shapes that can change the state of the neuron from excited to inhibited, or vice versa. For example, an incoming signal becomes weaker as it traverses a really long dendrite to the neuron body. A signal that travels along a short dendrite will be much more powerful when it hits the neuron body. In addition, it takes a higher dose of neurotransmitter to excite a fat neuron than to excite a small one.

The human brain contains approximately 100 billion to 200 billion neurons that fire about 10 million billion times per second. Each neuron connects to roughly 10,000 other neurons. This is how the brain handles trillions of operations per second. It's an extremely complex neural network.

A computer neural network is a simplified version of a biological neural network. In the biological form, a neuron accepts input from its dendrites and supplies output to other neurons through its axons. The neuron applies weights to the connections, or synapses, between dendrites and axons. A higher weight might be applied to a synapse related to touching fire than to a synapse about seeing the pretty color of fireball orange.

In the computerized version, each "input neuron" feeds information into every neuron in what is called the hidden layer, which may have one or many layers of neurons. If the hidden layer has two layers of neurons, for example, then every neuron in the first hidden layer feeds into every neuron in the second. Every neuron in the last hidden layer feeds into neurons in the output layer.

The designer of a neural net provides different weights for the connections among neurons. While our brain receives input from many sources, such as sensations on our skin, what we hear, what we smell, and so forth, an artificial neural network takes input only from values we provide, and then it weighs everything and supplies a best-guess answer.

Various methods exist for applying weights to artificial neurons, and for assembling the input, hidden, and output layers into network architectures. A neural network learns by adjusting the weights given to its neurons. A very common neural net architecture called back propagation compares forecasts to actuals, then adjusts the weighted interconnections among neurons. Over time, as it compares more forecasts to actuals, the neural weights become more accurate. In a sense, the neural net itself has learned and adjusted to its environment.

K. Eric Drexler believes that nanotechnology is required to achieve true artificial intelligence in our computer equipment, both hardware and software. He writes that "one can imagine AI hardware built to imitate a brain not only in function, but in structure. This might result from a neural-simulation approach, or from the evolution of AI programs to run on hardware with a brainlike style of organization. . . . [Speed and accuracy estimates are] crude, of course. A neural synapse is more complex than a switch; it can change its response to signals by changing its structure. Over time, synapses even form and disappear. These changes in the fibers and connections of the brain embody the long-term mental changes we call learning." He goes on to explain that "just as the molecular machinery of a synapse responds to patterns of neural activity by modifying the synapse's structure, so the nanocomputers will respond to patterns of activity by directing the nanomachinery to modify the switch's structure. With the right programming, and with communication among the nanocomputers to simulate chemical signals, such a device should behave almost exactly like a brain."[31]

While the human brain can direct computers to some extent, it seems unlikely that bottom-up AI software will run on (that is, operate on or inhabit/use) the neural circuitry of a human brain anytime soon.

However, if an AI is built using some sort of molecular

hardware backbone with nanotech components, then it's conceivable that the AI software can run on molecular fleshware, such as the neural networks in a human brain. If an anime character is an artificially intelligent robot, his mind (the AI component of his "brain") could transfer in some way to a humanoid made from flesh.

Research is already under way to create molecular-based computers. In fact, Stanley Williams, director of the Quantum Science Research group at Hewlett-Packard Labs, claims that "the age of computing hasn't even begun yet. We're still playing around in essentially Stone Age times technologically."[32]

For example, DNA computers have been in the works for years. In 1997, two researchers at the University of Rochester, Animesh Ray and Mitsu Ogihara, constructed logic gates using DNA molecules, a major step toward DNA computers capable of solving problems normally handled by digital computers.

Instead of using silicon chips and electrical currents, DNA computers rely on deoxyribonucleic acids as memory units and carry out fundamental operations by recombinant techniques. The main difference between DNA computers and electronic computers is that regular computer bits have two positions (on/off) while DNA bits have four (adenine, cytosine, guanine, and thymine). Therefore, DNA molecules can in theory handle any problem performed on a conventional computer, but can manage more complex operations as well by using their two extra positions.

Most electronic computers handle operations linearly—one operation at a time, if at incredible speeds. DNA computers rely on biochemical reactions that work in parallel. A single operation in a DNA computer can affect trillions of other DNA strands. DNA computers are thus much faster than any electronic computer.

Synthesized DNA strands are used in DNA computers. The amount of information that can be stored in these biological strands is staggering. One cubic centimeter of DNA material can hold as much as 1,021 bits of information. More to the point, it's estimated that one pound of synthetic DNA has the capacity to store more information than all the electronic computers in use in the world today.

If it's possible to create artificially intelligent robots with emotions, then aren't these creations human?

Let's think back to the questions Hideki asks about Chi in *Chobits:* If a computer's memories can be deleted, meaning that her memories aren't really her own, then can she be considered a person? Our answer: sure, because people forget things all the time. As we get older, for example, our memories fade; and quite often throughout life, we don't remember things as they actually happened. Does this lack of memory make us any less human?

Chobits also poses the question: after someone has been in love with a perfect humanoid Persocom—brilliant, beautiful, loving, giving in all ways—how can that person ever love a mere human again? Again, we answer: why not? People fall in and out of love all the time, and this doesn't mean that they cease to be people.

When a person falls in love, he or she often thinks the new lover is perfect: beautiful, kind, brilliant, and so forth. Over time, his or her love fades, and someone new comes along who attracts him or her the way the former lover did long before. It seems natural that a human could adore a Persocom, then fall in love with a human, then be attracted to another Persocom, then another human, and so forth.

Now let's talk about the human soul. Does the *Chobits* Persocom have a soul? The anime *Ghost in the Shell* asks: if an artificial intelligence generates its own soul, is the machine human or mere machine? Must you be born with a soul, or can you create your own? Just what is a soul?

It was the French philosopher René Descartes who wrote the famous line, "I think, therefore I am." Descartes was referring to the human ability to consider itself as a distinct individual, a self with a soul. But what is the soul, the self, the mind?[33] According to Plato, the gods inserted souls into our bodies. These souls were "of another nature,"[34] and inside digestive systems was "the part of the soul which desires meats and drinks and the other things of which it has need by reason of the bodily nature."[35]

Aristotle assumed that all objects consist of matter, and that the forms of objects change as this matter changes. For example, a house consists of stones, and when someone takes the stones apart, the house changes form. So to Aristotle, the soul is the "form" that a creature takes, and it takes care of and consists of everything that the creature does to stay alive. Aristotle thought that creatures other than humans have souls; that each type of creature has a different type of soul. A different set of conditions is required to keep a tiger alive than to keep a human alive, for example. However, he did think that the human soul differed from the animal soul in that the human soul was *rational* and included reason and will: the mind, the self, the consciousness.

There's no reason to think that an artificially intelligent machine can't have a soul, as defined by Aristotle. The artificially intelligent creature can be rational, have reason, and have its own will.

In the Old Testament, the soul lives in the blood and is life. It dies when the human dies. In the New Testament, the soul is immortal and will face either eternal bliss or eternal hell. In the early church, the Old Testament soul lived in the heart and liver, while the New Testament soul was invisible and lived nowhere and everywhere all at once, while somehow having special facilities inside the skull.

Long before scientists discovered atoms, the Greek philosopher Epicurus suggested that the world consisted of invisible particles that controlled almost everything. Perhaps the gods didn't care about humans at all; only the particles mattered. In addition, Epicurus postulated that the soul was made of atoms inside the chest, and these soul atoms seeped from our bodies, only to be restored as we breathed. The soul was, in essence, a cosmic property. When the soul seeped from the body but breath no longer replenished the soul atoms, that was the point where the human body died.

Of course, religious people were quite upset by the idea of a soul that didn't survive human death. In fact, Dante went so far as to put Epicurus in hell.

Along came Thomas Aquinas in the thirteenth century. Aquinas ignored Epicurus's claim that atoms and cosmic souls existed. Instead, the theologian suggested that the stars were a twinkling of heaven, where all good souls lived forever after the body died. Aquinas supported Aristotle's idea that the soul resides in the heart and is the "form" of all life. Aquinas also taught that the soul's facilities were in the skull, and that of all the animal souls, only the human soul survived death.

The battle has raged for centuries: religious soul versus philosophy versus science. Let's look at the question another way:[36] Each person may respond in an entirely different way to the same set of events. Each person uses free will to determine whether and how he or she will respond to a loud crash, to name one example. Our souls, our minds, require free will to operate. How does free will function within the laws of physics, which have rigid, deterministic laws?

Circuits supposedly operate in fixed ways: if A happens, do B; if B happens, trigger C and D. Is it possible that the mind plumbs the depths of brain cells and nerves to create the neurotransmissions that enable us to create new ideas and make decisions based on personal morals and private memories? Is the mental truly part of the physical brain, or does the mental operate in conjunction with—but separate from—the physical brain? These are key questions when considering whether a machine can have a soul; that is, whether a machine can be considered human.

We could assume that free will, the ability to be an individual self with an individual soul, is the force of consciousness. We don't know if monkeys are conscious (Lois believes they are), if worms, computers, and dogs are conscious. We don't know if a human baby is conscious an hour before birth, or three months before birth. Just when does a human become conscious? And who's to say that our dogs and cats aren't conscious and operating with free will? This factor doesn't mean that dogs, cats, and monkeys are humans. If computers are conscious, it doesn't imply that they're human, either; a computer with a so-called soul could still be considered a computer rather than a human, just as a monkey with a soul is still a monkey.

According to the dualist theory, we consist of a physical body and a soul or mind. The body is the host receptacle for the soul/mind. Descartes believed that the soul is based in the brain's pineal gland. It is through the pineal gland that the ephemeral mind interacts with the physical body.

As shamans and other spiritual seekers study, starve, and pray, it's possible for their souls to be released from the prisons of their bodies. In death, the soul is released to ultimate freedom.

Some philosophers have pegged the human body as a machine, with the soul guiding it. The soul is invisible and has no size or weight. If the human body is an engine, the soul has often been called "the ghost in the machine."[37] We're reminded of the name of a very popular anime, *Ghost in the Shell.*

If the soul is an invisible ghost, we're left to wonder *where it is.* Does it just float through the air surrounding our bodies? Does it cruise inside our bodies? It is far away in outer space? Is it in some fold of space-time, yet locked into the grids of our bodies? And if the soul does have substance, then we are left with similar questions: *where and what is it?*

If the soul is the essence of who we are, does it exist after our bodies die? Why would it? And how does the air around us contain the billions and billions of souls that were once attached to live humans? And where is the soul before we're born? Does it exist, or does it come into being the moment a human is born?

Today, neuroscientists are trying to map what happens from neuron to neuron as we see objects and work out math problems. But the idea of consciousness or self remains elusive. Possibly, as we suggested earlier, the soul or self is really a brain-wide synchrony; that is, if we feel happy, it means that complex bunches of neurons are interacting in some way. Consciousness may be part of the physical nature of our individual brains. In other words, it's not a distinctly different being that controls our brains, but just the collective way our brains function.

If this is the case, then a machine with an artificially intelligent mind can also be happy, conscious, and so on. A complex bunch of digital neurons can interact in such a way to make the computer *feel* alive. There's no reason a computer can't be considered a living creature—though, as noted earlier, this doesn't imply that the computer is *human*; rather, it simply means that it is a sentient being.

4. Colonies in Space

The Population Bomb

The population of Earth during the writing of this book (April 2005) stands at approximately 6,514,777,000 people. Thirty years from now, the population is estimated to rise to 10,000,000,000. The amount of habitable land on Earth isn't likely to change much; nor are our nonrenewable resources such as oil, natural gas, and coal likely to last much longer. Each year, our planet grows increasingly crowded. Sooner or later, a solution has to be found to this "population bomb" or humanity will sink back in on itself and self-destruct. Such is the premise of hundreds of dystopian future novels written over the past several decades, including such important works as *Stand on Zanzibar* and *The Sheep Look Up* by John Brunner, and *Make Room, Make Room,* by Harry Harrison, which was made into the film *Soylent Green.*

Fifty years ago, the solution to the problem of global overpopulation was thought to be the colonization of other planets and solar systems. There were numerous nonfiction books written by well-known scientists published on the conquest of space, life on Mars, and the colonization of the moon. There were articles in major magazines such as *Life* and *Look* about exploring other worlds, and TV shows like *Disneyland* devoted hours to specials on space stations and trips through the solar system. Unfortunately, as the years passed and we learned more about outer space from our missions to the moon and space probes sent to Mars and Venus, these optimistic visions began to fade. Venus was discovered to be a hothouse world with surface temperatures well over 500 degrees. And Mars was equally desolate, with nights far colder than a night on Antarctica.

Space stations—donut shapes filled with spiked hallways, rotating majestically 24,000 miles above the Earth—proved to be impractical. Transporting the necessary building materials to outer space was a much bigger and more expensive proposition than anyone had guessed. Plus, it turned out to be easier to send astronauts directly to the moon from Earth than to launch missions from space stations. Even if space stations had been practical, the number of people that could be supported on such rings would be minimal, and would in no way be able to help the population crisis on Earth. Novels like Arthur C. Clarke's *Islands in the Sky* and Murray Leinster's *Space Tug,* once considered as much fact as fiction, turned out to be more outrageous than novels predicting the end of civilization by a giant meteor strike.

Another science fiction concept dealing with the problem of overpopulation was the "generation starship." First discussed by SF writer Don Wilcox in a 1940 story called "The Voyage that Lasted Six Hundred Years," the notion was of a massive space ark sent to the stars at a speed nearly that of light. Even going that fast, it would take such a ship four years to reach the nearest star, and no one could predict how long it might take to find a habitable planet. Therefore, the ark was designed to serve as a small world for the crew, with generation after generation born on the ship, until a suitable planet is located. A similar idea was used by Robert A. Heinlein in his 1941 short novel *Universe.* In the Heinlein novel, after many generations have lived and died on the giant spaceship, the purpose of the voyage has been forgotten. Only when the huge spaceship comes to a habitable world do some of the people on board the star cruiser learn that the world isn't made of metal. Generation starships were an interesting concept for science fiction adventures, but were not the least bit practical in the real world. At least, no one has proposed these vehicles so far.

Perhaps the most ambitious plan to settle other planets that have atmospheres, such as Mars, is "terraforming." The word is credited to science fiction author Jack Williamson, who first used it in his 1942 story "Collision Course." The basic concept of terraforming is to transform a planet through vast engineering efforts into a habitat that would closely resemble that of Earth and thus be suitable for human life. In other words, terraforming Mars would be a planetary engineering project to turn Mars into a world where people could live without massive artificial life-support systems. This scenario plays out during a period of decades—or even centuries.

Terraforming is an idea that has enchanted science fiction authors for the past twenty years. Terraforming Mars, proponents contend, would provide an entirely new world to settle and thus relieve the population overflow on Earth. Many people argue, however, that Mars would fill up faster than anyone imagines—and what next after Mars? Terraforming Mars would be an engineering project of global proportions and would challenge humanity like no other event in history; furthermore, it would require technology significantly more advanced than what we have today. Even terraforming advocates admit it would take a minimum of two hundred years to modify Mars to the stage where even simple anaerobic microorganisms and algae could survive.[38] Whether such a challenge would wipe out all of Earth's natural resources in an impossible project or save humanity from destruction for the next thousand years is a question that has not yet been answered by those few who believe the task possible. It does seem unlikely the project will be started anytime in the near future.

Still, even if we assumed that Mars could be terraformed quickly, the numbers still don't promise long-term relief. Remaking Mars into a second Earth would double the land area presently available to humankind. That's a good short-term solution, but as we mentioned before, Earth's population is growing fast. It's estimated that the number of people on Earth will double in forty years. Which makes the Mars solution seem a lot less long-term than had been hoped.

Colonies on the moon are certainly possible, and it seems likely that such outposts will be established sometime in the next century. Unfortunately, the moon is a dead world without the necessary resources to support a large independent human colony. All of the start-up materials would have to be rocketed to the moon from Earth. However, Robert A. Heinlein did write a convincing novel about life on a moon colony titled *The Moon Is a Harsh Mistress*. It also pointed the way to a possible solution for Earth's population crisis. Why not settle the billions of extra people born in the next few centuries in the vast emptiness of outer space? It's not as crazy as it sounds.

The *Gundam* World

We discussed the *Gundam* anime series in terms of mecha in chapter 2. Now, let's take a look at them in relation to the settlement of outer space. As mentioned previously, *Mobile Suit*

Gundam was a televised anime written and directed by Tomino Yoshiyuki that ran for forty-three episodes in Japan in 1979. The series didn't receive high ratings when it first aired. As often happens with anime shows, it was even cancelled before the actual series was scheduled to end. The show had been designed to run for fifty-two episodes, and programmers were instructed to cut it back to thirty-nine. Fortunately, the producers of the show were able to keep it running through forty-three episodes.

The series is extremely important to anime historians in that Yoshiyuki broke new ground in the giant-robot field. As explained in chapter 2, before *Gundam*, robot shows were little more than weekly battles between the good giant robot and evil space invaders or inter-dimensional aliens. Early audiences who were expecting another giant robot show instead found the first work of anime in an entirely new genre—the mecha drama, or the "real robot" genre as opposed to the "super robot" genre. In *Gundam*, the featured robots were mechanical devices piloted by humans and used by characters both good and evil. Equally important, the future world in which *MSG* took place was a fully developed civilization with a history and with characters who were neither all good nor all evil, but a mix of both.

The series did very well in reruns, and three compilation films edited for theatrical release in 1981 were big hits. The toy models based on the Gundam suits from the show sold very well, pleasing the sponsor of the series. Like many innovative shows, the series didn't connect with a loyal audience until it was shown a second time. New versions of the *Gundam* saga continued to play well on Japanese TV for the next fifteen years.

The basic idea of the "mobile suit" as a weapon came from the high-powered space suit used in the novel *Starship Troopers* by Robert A. Heinlein. The rest of the story bore little resemblance to the Heinlein book. Yasuhiko Yoshikazu did the character designs and Okawara Kunio was responsible for the mechanical designs, including the titular giant robot, the RX-78-2 Gundam.

In an interview conducted around that time, Tomino said, "As a creator, I did not find any need to tell any more stories about Gundam. But as a producer, I had no choice. The audiences demanded it. But I did not like it." This annoyance with his characters resulted in a number of them being killed in major battles in later series. Tomino's habit of wiping out large sections of his cast at the end of story lines resulted in his nickname "Kill 'Em All!"

The basic backstory of all of the Gundam series delves into the problem raised in the first section of this chapter. It is decades in the future and there are billions more people alive. These people need a place to live in peace, eat and drink, work, fall in love, marry, and die. They need a homeland where none exists. So they set out on a mission to build their homeland in the middle of nowhere.

To escape an increasingly overcrowded Earth, world leaders gather together and pool their resources to construct giant cylindrical space colonies, called "sides," which can indefinitely sustain millions of space-dwelling humans. When humanity takes to space, they mark this new phase of human endeavor with a new calendar. They start numbering this new Universal Century calendar with the beginning of the exodus to the outer space colonies. Thus, U.C. 01 is the first year humankind lives in space. The colonization of space continues from that point in history for the next fifty years. With the passage of decades, Earth succeeds in transplanting most of its population to space.

In the Universal Century timeline, space colonies are established at the five Earth-sun Lagrangian points. Since these spots are vast spheres of space, these Lagrangian points are home to numerous space colonies. Individual colonies are known as "bunches," and a group of colonies that occupy a Lagrangian point are known collectively, as mentioned above, as a "side." Because several sides sometimes share a single Lagrangian point, it is possible to have two sides in close orbit to one another. All colonies in the Universal Century are O'Neill "Island 3" type colony cylinders, except for the "close-type" colonies of Side 3. Fans of the *MSG* universe have identified eight sides and at least sixteen bunches in the U.C. timeline.

The first fifty years of the Universal Century are spent building the various colonies and placing them at Lagrangian points, as well as colonizing the moon. By U.C. 50, nine billion of the eleven billion people in the Earth Federation live in space colonies or on the moon. While this sounds like an incredible number, it has actually been estimated that if we built such space habitats using only the resources of the asteroid belt, humankind could construct space colonies with three thousand times the living space available on Earth.

Mobile Suit Gundam is a typical story of rebellion of colonies from the mother country. But in this case, the colonies are located in outer space and the mother country is Earth itself. The space-born members of the Federation, called spacenoids, are anxious to be free from the tyrannical rule of Earth Federation. A powerful group of colonies, Side 3, under the leadership of Zeon Zum Daikun, plot to break free from the federation. While they avoid any confrontation with Earth forces, the leaders of Side 3 change the name of their collection of colonies to the Republic of Zeon. When Daikun dies under mysterious circumstances, his advisor, Degin Sodo Zabi, takes control of the Zeon government and renames the group the Duchy of Zeon.

Under Zabi's rule, Zeon turns into a militaristic state. On January 3, U.C. 79, the Duchy of Zeon declares a war of independence against the Earth Federation. Three seconds after making this declaration, Zeon launches massive attacks on the space colonies at Sides 1, 2, and 4. Zeon forces bombard the Federation fleets stationed at these sides with nuclear weapons and pump poison gas into the colonies' air-filtration plants. The Federation spaceships are destroyed. Around 2.8 billion people are killed by the Zeon's deadly gas and nuclear attacks.

In an attempt to bring the war to a quick close, the forces of Zeon attach giant motors to one of the now-lifeless colonies and rocket it out of orbit. This plan is known as Operation British.

The Zeon forces intend to drop the twenty-mile-long cylinder onto the Federation's headquarters at Jaburo in South America. The Earth Federal Forces intercept the falling colony, but are unable to stop it. The colony breaks up upon re-entering the Earth's atmosphere, and pieces crash down across the world. The largest chunk hits Sydney, Australia. The impact kills 200 million people and destroys one-sixth of the Australian continent.

Over half the human race is killed within the first days of what becomes known as the "One Year War." The violence continues to escalate when Zeon makes a second attempt to drop an orbital colony on Jaburo. This time, however, the Earth Federation forces are ready, and a huge outer space battle takes place. Nuclear missiles are launched and the population of Side 5 is wiped out— another 2.5 billion people killed.

With over five billion humans killed in the early days of the One Year War, the two sides in the conflict agree to the Antarctica Treaty, which bans gas weapons, nuclear weapons, and colony drops in the conflict. Meanwhile, both armies convert mobile suits—mechanized construction suits used to build the space colonies—into war machines. The discovery of subatomic Minovsky particles makes it possible to power the suits with compact thermonuclear reactors. The Minovsky particles emitted by these mobile suit reactors have an unusual side effect. The particles jam all conventional radar, essentially rendering the suits invisible to most spaceships. Thus these mobile suits usher in a new form of close space combat.

As the first *Mobile Suit Gundam* anime begins, Zeon and the Federation are getting ready for a new round of battles. Zeon has captured a number of areas on Earth, including much of Asia, Europe, and North America. The Federation has a powerful space armada and controls the rest of Earth from its base in South America. With the forces nearly equally balanced, whoever develops the best mobile suit will most likely win the war.

This, then, is the world of *Mobile Suit Gundam*, the most detailed space opera ever broadcast in Japan. The series is considered one of the high points in modern anime. In chapter 2, we list various anime series that comprise the *Gundam* saga. There are numerous other *Mobile Suit Gundam* adventures that take place in alternate universes. As the science used in those series is the same as that of *Mobile Suit Gundam*, we'll restrict our investigation to the original *MSG* universe.

Lagrangian Points

The basic scientific concept in the *MSG* universe is that humanity has been able to create artificial colonies in space that provide all the necessities of civilization. These colonies are inhabited by billions of people, thus solving the problem of the population bomb. Equally important is the fact that the colonies are entirely self-supporting, and thus do not require a steady influx of natural resources from Earth. It's this independence, of course, that also propels the plot of the series. Since the colonies are no longer dependent on Earth, why shouldn't they govern themselves and keep the goods and products they produce? In many ways, the *MSG* universe follows the story of the American Revolution, but with much more deadly technology.

What's most important to us is the question of whether such space colonies are possible, even several hundred years in the future. It's a question that pertains not only to the believability of this particular anime, but to continued life on Earth in the twenty-third or twenty-fourth century. As mentioned, there are no inhabitable planets in our solar system. Establishing a base on Mars would require massive fleets of spaceships from Earth traveling for years, a plan that at this time seems impractical. Terraforming Mars would take decades, if not centuries—without guaranteed results. Establishing orbital colonies would be expensive but possible, and hopefully such colonies would pay back their investment over the years.

But to fully answer the question, we must first know what Lagrangian points are and why they are so important to space colonies.

The first requirement for any relatively safe space colony is that it stay in place relative to Earth. If nothing else, a relatively stable position would mean that travel between Earth and the colony would be comparatively easy by spaceship. Also, by maintaining the same position in relation to Earth, it would also retain the same position in relation to the sun. This would be extremely important if crops are to be grown on the satellite; the inhabitants would sleep at night, much like on the mother planet. In addition, a great deal of information could be learned about space by a satellite observing changes in magnetic fields and particle flows from one fixed spot.

Unfortunately, keeping a satellite fixed above a certain space cannot be done. To remain in space and at the same time resist Earth's gravity, a satellite must always be moving in a prescribed orbit. At present, the best we can do is put a satellite above a spot on the equator and make sure its motion matches the rotation of Earth. In that manner, the satellite can stay above the same spot.

There is, however, another method by which a satellite can keep a fixed position relative to Earth. A powerful spaceship can break free from Earth's gravity and enter an orbit around the sun (just like the planets). If the ship orbits the sun in the same period of time that Earth does[39], i.e., one year, it would keep a fixed position relative to Earth. This concept has been studied by NASA scientists because if the satellite position is between the sun and Earth, the spacecraft can be used as an "early warning system" for solar flares and changes in the solar winds.

Unfortunately, as discovered by Johannes Kepler in 1619, orbital laws require objects like planets and satellites closer to the sun to move faster. Earth revolves around the sun in 365 days, but Venus, much closer to the sun, revolves around the sun in 225 days, while Mercury's orbit is only 88 days. Therefore any spaceship orbiting the sun that is closer to the sun than it is to Earth would have a revolution period shorter than that of Earth. And it would not remain in a fixed spot over Earth.

However, gravitation provides a loophole. If our spacecraft is placed between the sun and Earth, Earth's gravity pulls it toward itself and cancels some of the pull of the sun. With a weaker pull toward the sun, the spacecraft then needs less speed to maintain its orbit. If the distance is just right—about four times the distance to the moon or 1/100 the distance to the sun—the spacecraft, too, will need just one year to go around the sun, and will keep its position between the sun and Earth. That position is the Lagrangian point L1, named after the Italian-French mathematician who pointed it out, Joseph-Louis Lagrange (1736–1813).

The L1 point is an excellent spot for monitoring the solar wind, which reaches it about one hour before it reaches Earth. In 1978 the International Sun-Earth Explorer-3 (ISEE-3) was launched toward L1, where it conducted such observations for several years.

Another Lagrangian point, L2, exists at about the same distance from Earth, but on the night side away from the sun. A spacecraft placed there is more distant from the sun and therefore should orbit it more slowly than Earth does; but the extra pull of Earth's gravity adds to the sun's pull, and this allows the spacecraft to move faster and keep up with Earth. The L2 point has been chosen by NASA as the future site of a large infrared observatory.

In all, there exist five Lagrangian points in the sun-Earth system, and such points also exist in the Earth-moon system.

Among these, the most attention has been given to the two stable points L4 and L5, located in the moon's orbit but off the position of the moon. These positions have been studied as possible sites for artificial space colonies, in the real world as well as in the distant imaginary future of *Mobile Suit Gundam*.

How did Kepler calculate the exact point in space where Earth's and the sun's gravity would create a stable orbital point? The work involves fairly detailed mathematics calculations, but nothing as difficult as calculus. In the interest of examining the science of anime, let's take a somewhat abbreviated look at his calculations.

We first assume that all orbits are circles. Then we go through the standard derivation of Kepler's third law for circular orbits.

In our calculations, we use the following shorthand:

- the gravitational constant will be denoted by G
- the mass of the sun will be denoted by M
- the mass of Earth will be denoted by m
- Earth's distance from the sun will be denoted by r
- the velocity of the Earth in its orbit will be denoted by v

By applying known facts about gravity and centripetal and centrifugal forces, we deduce that:
$$GMm/r^2 = mv^2/r:$$
If we multiply both sides by r/m, we end up with:
$$GM/r = v^2:$$

Now, if we say that T is the orbital period, since the distance covered by Earth on each orbit is $2r\pi$, then $vT = 2r\pi$. (Remember this equation for later.) If we divide both sides by T, the resultant equation looks like this:

$$v = 2\pi r/T$$

If we square each side of the equation, we find that $v^2 = 4\pi^2 r^2/T^2$. Therefore:

$$GM/r = v^2 = 4\pi^2 r^2/T^2$$

Let's divide both sides by r^2. We end up with an equation that looks like this:

$$GM/r^3 = 4\pi^2/T^2$$

If we multiply both sides by $r^3 T^2$ we arrive at $GMT^2 = 4r^3\pi^2$. With G, M, 4, and π all being constants, we have Kepler's third law: The square of the orbital period of a planet is proportional to the cube of the mean distance from the sun.

Remember, r is the distance between the sun and Earth. Next, let's consider a spaceship of mass *mss* (for mass of space ship) that is somewhere on the path between Earth and the sun. If the spaceship is located a distance *R* from Earth, it would therefore be (r – R) distance from the sun. Now, the force, *F,* that is pulling the spaceship toward the sun is decreased by the pull of Earth, which is tugging on it in the opposite direction. We can write this out in an equation like this:

$$F = GM(mss)/(r{-}R)^2 - Gm(mss)/R^2$$

Now let us assume the spaceship moves in a circle around the sun, with a velocity we call *vss* (velocity of the spaceship). The centrifugal forces balance the force of the attraction toward the sun by the equation:

$$GM(mss)/(r{-}R)^2 - Gm(mss)/R^2 = (mss)(vss)^2/(r{-}R)$$

If we multiply this entire equation by $(r{-}R)/mss$, we get

$$GM/(r{-}R) - Gm(r{-}R)/R^2 = (vss)^2$$

Now, if we assume that the spaceship is moving around the sun in a circle, it does so at the radius $(r - R)$. Of course, that means Earth must always be in the right spot in space to pull the rocket away from the sun. We will deal with that problem in a minute.

The orbital period of the spaceship, *tss*, can be put into one of our previous equations to look like this:

$$(vss)(tss) = 2\pi(r{-}R) \text{ (where } r - R \text{ is the distance}$$
$$\text{the ship is from the Sun)}$$

Squaring both sides of the equation and doing a quick division, we arrive at:

$$(vss)^2 = 4\pi^2 (r{-}R)^2 /(tss)^2$$

Since we have two equations with $(vss)^2$, some quick substitution results in the following equation:

$$GM/(r{-}R) - Gm(r{-}R)/R^2 = 4\pi^2 (r{-}R)^2/(tss)^2$$

Noticing that $(r - R)$ is in both sides of the equation, we divide everything by $(r - R)^2$ and reduce our equation to:

$$GM/(r{-}R)^3 - Gm/R^2(r{-}R) = 4\pi^2/(tss)^2$$

Looking at this equation, we note that it closely resembles Kepler's third equation, except that Earth's opposing pull is now added into the calculations. The one question, as noted above, is this: will

Earth always be located where its pull on the spaceship is exactly opposite from that of the sun? The answer is no. Not unless the two orbital periods are the same. In other words, if tss = T.

That occurs only when the spaceship's motion matches that of Earth and the distance between the two remains constant. In general that just happens at one value of R. That's the point we want to find.

If we assume tss = T, the two relations with $4\pi^2/T^2$ on the right side are identical, which means we can work out an equation to find R. That equation, after some mathematical manipulation, turns out to be:

$$GM/(r-R)^3 - Gm/R^2(r-R) = GM/r^3$$

We need to solve for R. If we divide both sides by GM, then G disappears entirely from the equation, and in place of the masses (*m*) of Earth, and (*M*) of the sun, we are left with only *their ratio*, which we will call *y*. In other words, y = m/M = (once we plug in the two masses and calculate) 3/1,000,000.

So our equation has been reduced to:

$$1/(r-R)^3 - y/R^2(r-R) = 1/r^3$$

If we multiply both sides by r^3 we get:

$$r^3/(r-R)^3 - y\, r^3/R^2(r-R) = 1$$

Now, doing a little fancy footwork, we multiply everything by 1, which we write as:

$$(1/\, r^3)/(1/r^3)$$

For simplicity's sake, we call the ratio R/r as z. Which translates our equation into:

$$1/(1-z)^3 - y/z^2(1-z) = 1$$

We need to solve for z, which in turn will give us R. The equation above is quite complicated, and finding an answer is nearly impossible. However, since we know that R (the distance of our ship from Earth) is very small compared to r (the distance of Earth to the sun), z is obviously quite small.

Now, knowing that z is very small, we can use some basic mathematics concerning approximate numbers. One such theorem says that if z is very small, then $(1 - z)(1 + z) = 1 - z^2$ can be written as $(1 - z)(1 + z) \sim 1$ where $\sim$ means "approximately." If we divide both sides by $(1 - z)$, we also come up with

$$(1+z) \sim 1/(1- z)$$

If z^2 is extremely small, and can be dropped in approximations, we can conclude:

$$1/(1-z)^3 \sim 1 + 3z$$

and:

$$[y/z^2]/(1-z) \sim [y/z^2] (1+z)$$

If we substitute these approximations into our first equation, we discover:

$$1 + 3z - [y/z^2] (1+z) \sim 1$$

which leads us to:

$$3z^3 \sim y(1+z)$$

Since both sides are extremely small, $(1 + z) \sim 1$ and our equation turns into:

$$3z^3 \sim y = 3/1,000,000$$

therefore:

$$z^3 \sim 1/1,000,000$$

If we take the cube root of both sides, we get:

R/r = z ~ 1/100 = 0.01

Which in simple terms means that the distance from Earth to the first Lagrangian point is approximately 0.01 the distance to the sun. To find the distance to the second Lagrangian point, we use r + R in our equations other than r − R; and, in the equation involving F, we add the terms instead of subtracting them since the gravity of the sun and Earth are both pulling in the same manner.

Calculating the positions of all five Lagrangian points would fill up too much of this book, so we'll leave it to the interested reader to follow up on the math. Having completed the derivation of the first point, we'll accept that the other points can be shown to be stable.

It is worth mentioning that Lagrangian points exist for every planet of the solar system that has one or more moons. Stable Lagrangian points are of great interest to astronomers because lots of stuff accumulates there. Take, for example, the Trojan asteroids of Jupiter. At present, nearly 1,700 asteroids called "Trojans" have been found orbiting the stable Lagrangian points of Jupiter's orbit around the sun. The first of these was discovered by the German astronomer Max Wolf in 1906, using a technique he invented in which he compared two photographs taken on different nights to see if any of the so-called stars in the pictures had moved. It proved quite successful, and Wolf discovered lots of asteroids. The first Trojan he discovered is called 588 Achilles, since it was the 588th asteroid found.

There have also been asteroids discovered at the L4 and L5 Lagrangian points of Mars and Neptune. No asteroids have yet been discovered at the Lagrangian points of Earth, but astronomers have noted huge clouds of cosmic dust at the L4 and L5 points.

With five stable points in outer space that are suitable for space colonies, what sort of colonies would be most practical for those locations? And would those colonies be the types used in the *MSG* universe? We'll explore those questions in our next section.

O'Neill Space Colonies

The man most responsible for the development of the space colony idea was Gerard K. O'Neill (1927–1992), a scientist at Princeton University's Institute for Advanced Study. Before investigating settling outer space, O'Neill was already well known as a high-energy physics researcher and inventor.

Fascinated by the notion of colonies in space, O'Neill asked a famous friend and fellow scientist, Freeman Dyson, if anyone had explored the idea before. Dyson pointed out the writings of Konstantin Tsiolkovsky, J. D. Bernal, and Dandridge Cole. Dyson himself had also written about settling space in a paper in which he described an artificial sphere in outer space totally surrounding a sun to collect all of its energy (this became known as a "Dyson sphere").[40]

Tsiolkovsky was an early Russian space scientist. In 1929 he wrote an article about "orbital mansion/greenhouses" that spun about to produce gravity and took full advantage of continuous sunlight in outer space. Bernal was another scientist who wrote about humankind building gigantic spheres orbiting Earth, while Cole came up with the notion of hollowing out asteroids for future space colonies.

In 1969, O'Neill was teaching a physics course at Princeton. The United States was in the midst of the Apollo space program, so O'Neill tried to use space travel in many of the physics assignments he gave to the class. Years later, he wrote that he was unhappy that so many of his students felt that a decline in the standard of living throughout the world was inevitable and that strict government regulation of resources would soon take place. He also was concerned about the problem of overpopulation, which fueled both of these concerns.

In one lesson, O'Neill asked his students the following: Is the surface of Earth really the best place for an expanding technological civilization? After doing some research, the answer appeared to be "no, it's not." Instead, working together, they designed an Earth-like space colony. After calculating the maximum size possible given the strengths of steel cable, aluminum plates, and glass panels at the time, they were surprised by their results. The conclusions reached by this class project were included in a 1974 article written by O'Neill published in *Physics Today*.

Studies funded by NASA reached the same conclusion: space habitats were actually possible using materials already available through modern technology. NASA scientists came up with several highly defined colony designs. The first design was known as Island One, or Bernal Sphere. Sunlight was reflected by two ring-shaped rows of windows at either end of the satellite. Agriculture took place in the outer anchor rings of the sphere. The Bernal Sphere was designed to be one kilometer in circumference. It was estimated it could support 10,000 people.

The second design, for Island Two, was shaped like a medicine capsule, and sunlight came through three windows running the length of the cylinder. Designed to be 1.8 kilometers in diameter, it could support 140,000 people.

Island Three was designed to take Island Two to the limit. It was to be a cylinder 6.4 kilometers (about 4 miles) in diameter and 32 kilometers (20 miles) long. With 4 miles of atmosphere, Island Three would have a blue sky overhead and even clouds.[41] Thus rainstorms would occur naturally. This third island would have more than 400 square kilometers of living space, enough to support 10 million people.

Other designs were developed as well, but Island Three was considered the limit of what could work economically. Theoretically, the largest space settlement using building materials then available was 19 kilometers (roughly 12 miles) in diameter, providing over 1,000 square miles of usable land.

O'Neill Island Three space habitats make a perfect background for the *Mobile Suit Gundam* universe, especially since the series references asteroids as an important part of the space colony universe. Hauling the necessary materials to build O'Neill space settlements to outer space would cost trillions of dollars. However, obtaining the necessary components from the moon or nearby asteroids would be financially feasible. A pound of ore from the moon could be transported to a Lagrangian point for 5 percent of the energy it would cost to rocket it from Earth to the same location.

Which raises the question of whether there is enough of the right types of raw materials on the moon to build our space colonies. From the Apollo missions, we know the lunar soil to be 40 percent oxygen, 20 percent silicon, 12 percent aluminum, 4 to 10 percent iron, 6 percent titanium, and 3 to 6 percent magnesium. Oxygen could be used for breathing, making water, and making rocket fuel. The silicon could be used to make glass and solar cells. The metals could be used in structural materials, as aluminum and titanium are popular in the aerospace industry for their combination of strength and light weight. Titanium is also a good high-temperature metal. Making fiberglass, cement, and ceramics from lunar materials has also been researched. Carbon, hydrogen, nitrogen, and most other elements necessary for building space settlements can be found in most asteroids.

What exactly does an O'Neill Island Three space settlement look like? It consists of two counter-rotating cylinders each 4 miles in diameter and 20 miles long. Each of the two cylinders has six equal-size stripes that run the length of the cylinder. Three of the stripes are windows. Three are the land areas.

Given that description, how do the colonies operate? The two cylinders rotate to provide simulated gravity on their inside surfaces. Normal Earth gravity would be achieved by rotating the colony at a rate of one revolution per 114 seconds. NASA experiments have shown that only a few people would experience motion sickness as a result of this rotation because of Coriolis effects in their inner ears. However, inhabitants would be able to detect spinward and antispinward directions by turning their heads. Cylinders containing this much air along with the aluminum walls of the colony would shield the inhabitants from cosmic rays. The interior of the cylinder would have three inhabited areas, each containing lakes, towns, farms, and so on.

On the back of each stripe of window would be large hinged mirrors. The unhinged edge of the windows would be aimed toward the sun. The mirrors would reflect sunlight into the cylinders through the windows. Night would be provided by completely opening the windows to view empty space. Doing this would also let heat radiate into space. During the daytime, the sun would move as the mirrors move, making it seem as though the sun were moving across the sky. A large parabolic collector at one end of the cylinder would focus solar energy into steam-driven generators, which would provide the colony's electricity.

Unfortunately, there's one flaw in the *MSG* universe that is never really addressed in the show. There are eight sides mentioned, and eighteen bunches. With each bunch consisting of two cylinders, the total population per bunch would be approximately 20,000,000 people. Eighteen bunches would support 360,000,000 people. Unfortunately, that's not nearly enough space settlers to affect the population bomb on Earth. Besides, according to the *MSG* history, when Zeon attackers killed the population of Sides 1, 2, and 4 with poison gas and nuclear weapons, supposedly 2.8 billion people were killed. That works out to more than 900 million people per side. Or over fifty bunches per side. Still, Lagrangian points are pretty huge, and with computers directing traffic and motion around the points, it's possible that there are a lot more bunches per side than were ever mentioned in the series.

While O'Neill space habitats exist only in the fictional worlds of *Mobile Suit Gundam* and *Babylon 5,* they are feasible, and many people believe they are the next great step to the stars for humanity. There is an L-5 Society devoted to living in space and numerous Web sites that feature long articles about the possibility of O'Neill colonies being developed over the next century. They are well worth investigating.

Minovsky Particles

The third scientific principle supporting the *MSG* universe is the "Minovsky particle." According to the series, a scientist named

Dr. Minovsky developed a new cold-fusion reactor that didn't emit stray neutrons. Without radiation, this new reactor was based on combining an isotope of helium, helium-3, with deuterium atoms, thereby releasing a large amount of energy in addition to converting the H3 isotope to helium-4 and a single proton. The new reactor was called the Minovsky-Ionesco, honoring one of the supporters of cold fusion reactions in the late twentieth century.

Approximately a decade later, researchers discovered that the cold fusion reaction produced a new atomic particle, which they named the "Minovsky particle." Researching this particle, these scientists soon learned that when charged, these Minovsky particles combined to form what they called an I-field. This field interfered with all sorts of communication devices, including radar. Within a short time, miniature Minovsky-Ionesco reactors were being used to power mobile weapon suits. Not only did the small reactor provide the necessary energy to run the combat armor, but the I-field made the suit invisible to electronic detection.

It's a fascinating idea, but unlike Lagrangian points and O'Neill space colonies, the science isn't real. Cold fusion has been a popular field of study for years, particularly in Japan, but has never been clearly demonstrated to be possible. Minovsky particles do not exist, nor are there any subatomic I-fields that block radar. However, not everything about Minovsky particles is untrue.

Helium-3 does exist, and it is an isotope of normal helium, which means it has the same atomic number as helium (the same number of protons: two) but with a different number of neutrons (one) in its nucleus. Helium-3 has been fused with deuterium to form helium-4, a single proton and energy. This reaction is much more containable than the neutrons produced in most fusion reactions, since protons are much easier to contain using magnetic and electrostatic fields. As we develop better fusion techniques, supplies of helium-3 could become quite valuable as a source of cheap energy.

As mentioned in the various *MSG* series, helium-3 is extremely rare on Earth. It is available on the moon in somewhat greater amounts than on Earth, and on Jupiter in much larger amounts. In *MSG* shows, space fleets are routinely sent to Jupiter to collect helium-3. That may someday also happen in the real world. But not yet.

Still, atomic reactions aren't the only reason scientists are interested in helium-3. The 1996 Nobel Prize Committee awarded the Nobel Prize in Physics to Douglas D. Osheroff, Robert C. Richardson, and David M. Lee for their discovery of the superfluid version of helium-3 in 1972.[42] A superfluid is a fluid that exhibits a frictionless flow at temperatures close to absolute zero.

Helium, as mentioned above, has two isotopes. These isotopes have very different properties. Helium-4 has a nucleus with two protons and two neutrons (the "4" stands for the total number of protons and neutrons). This nucleus is surrounded by an electron shell with two electrons. The number of particles constituting this atom is even, which makes helium-4 a boson.

The nucleus of helium-3 also has two protons, but only one neutron (thus the 3). Since its electron shell also has two electrons, helium-3 consists of an odd number of particles, which is known as a fermion. Since the two isotopes of helium are built of different numbers of particles, dramatic differences in their behavior arise when they are cooled to temperatures near absolute zero.

At the beginning of the 1970s, Lee, Osheroff, and Richardson discovered, in the low-temperature laboratory at Cornell University, that helium-3 could be made superfluid at a temperature only about two-thousandths of a degree above absolute zero. This superfluid quantum liquid differed greatly from the helium-4 isotope, which had been discovered in the 1930s and studied at about 2 degrees (i.e., a thousand times) higher temperature. The new quantum liquid helium-3 had very special characteristics. One thing those characteristics demonstrated was that the quantum laws of microphysics sometimes directly govern the behavior of macroscopic bodies as well.

Even more interesting is that the phase transitions to superfluidity in helium-3 have recently been involved in several experiments concerning string theory. These immense hypothetical strings may have formed the universe as a result of the rapid-phase transitions believed to have taken place a fraction of a second after the big bang. Research teams used neutrino-induced nuclear reactions to heat their superfluid helium-3 samples locally and rapidly. When these were cooled again, balls of vortices were formed. It is these vortices that are presumed to correspond to the cosmic strings. Though the results do not prove that string theory is correct,[43] they do seem to support the possibility.

Who knows? Perhaps in twenty years, we'll all be watching *Mobile Suit Gundam: String Theory Adventures.*

5. Policing an Anime Future

It's a Cyberpunk World

It's the year 2029, a little less than a quarter of a century from today. The world has undergone some incredible changes, but it has also remained the same in many ways. The future is a mixture of the past and the present. Many of the differences in the world are extremely subtle, while others are startling. We recognize the changes, but we're not sure we understand them. Or like them. The future isn't exactly what we expect. But then, it never is.

The series we're watching is called *Ghost in the Shell: Stand Alone Complex,* and its history is as complicated as that of most soap operas. The series has deep roots in modern science fiction as well as in anime and manga. *Ghost in the Shell* was written as a manga by Masamune Shirow and appeared in print in 1991. In 1995, the manga was somewhat loosely adapted into the anime movie *Ghost in the Shell* by Mamoru Oshii. It was a hit in Japan but did not fare as well in the rest of the world, due to its slow-moving story line and lack of action.

The anime and the manga both dealt with the near future on Earth and what it means to be human in a world filled with artificial intelligence, intelligent machines, and cyborgs. We've already discussed the AI part of the show in chapter 3, along with our thoughts on the concept of the soul. A TV series of *Ghost in the Shell: Stand Alone Complex* was produced in 2002. It consisted of twenty-six episodes, which, unlike most manga, did not connect into one long story line. Instead, the show was more like a modern-day police drama, with the same cast of special agents battling a variety of futuristic crimes. About half of the episodes involved an ongoing plot line dealing with a super-hacker cyber-criminal known as "The Laughing Man." The villain's name is a reference taken directly from the works of American author J. D. Salinger.

Further complicating the show's history is the fact that while the same characters appeared in the film and the TV show, the

TV show took place in an alternate reality different from that of the movie. At the end of the film, the heroine undergoes a startling transformation, as her intelligence combines with that of a computer. That event, and everything leading up to it, never occurred in the TV show, which features the heroine as the lead character.

Just to make things more confusing, a new *Ghost in the Shell* movie, *Innocence*, was released in 2004. It tied in directly with the first movie and had little to do with the TV series. However, in 2004, a new TV series started running in Japan—*Ghost in the Shell: Stand Alone Complex, The Second GIG*, which tied in directly to the first season of the TV show.

The future in the various *Ghost in the Shell* components is a dark, cybernetic vision of our world twenty-five years from now. *Ghost* focuses on a covert operations section of the Japanese National Public Safety Commission, Section 9, which specializes in fighting technology-related crime. In the future, most people are cyborgs—that is, humans beings with machine enhancements. Some humans, including Major Motoko Kusanagi (a woman, for those not familiar with Japanese names), have totally artificial bodies. The "ghost" of the story refers to the spirit, or the soul, of individuals, which, in this future time, can be transferred from body to body, from artificial cyborg unit to cyborg unit. Thus, the Major actually is a "ghost" in a shell.

In this future, nearly all humans are connected to a planet-wide virtual-reality net that they can hook into using implants in their bodies. The agents for Section 9 can "jack in" to a network that enables them, among other things, to communicate telepathically and to access data archives. Those agents with totally cyborg bodies are able to perform superhuman feats of strength, speed, and agility.

One of the main themes of the TV series is Kusanagi's confusion as to whether she is a real person or merely a part of a machine. Complicating things are her relationships with other team members: Bateau, who is another cyborg being, a strongman with just a hint of his human body remaining; and Togusa, whose body is totally human. Another underlying theme of the series is what results from the merging of man and technology and how the Internet, with its unlimited communication opportunities, is changing the nature of human interaction.

Another intriguing concept developed in the movie and the TV show is cybernetic warfare. In the dark future of *GIS*, super-hackers use the Internet to hack into the cybernetic section of other people's brains. Having done so, the hacker can feed false information into a person's memory or cause their senses to go haywire. Worse, a cyber-criminal can rewrite or even destroy memories in the other person's brain.

This cybernetic warfare is only possible because of the links that exist between humans and cyberspace in the world of *GIS*. It's made clear a number of times that the one sure way a person can stop criminals from hacking into his or her memories is to disconnect from the Internet. Yet, in the show, even those most directly affected by such cybernetic attacks refuse to let go of their network. In that sense, *Ghost in the Shell* describes a possible next step in human evolution. We discuss this idea in chapter 6.

What makes *Ghost in the Shell* so fascinating is the depth and complexity of the world Shirow created. In the English version of the manga, the footnotes and commentary by the author on the technology and the political and social background for the story takes up thirty pages. Shirow acknowledges in these notes that his concept of "ghost" to define the human consciousness or soul comes from British author Arthur Koestler's extremely dense study of human thought, *The Ghost in the Machine.*

The future as described by Shirow and then further imagined by Mamoru in the film is a vivid example of a subgenre of science fiction literature known as cyberpunk. Cyberpunk is centered around computer technology and the breakdown of normal society in the near future. Unlike the utopias of earlier science fiction, the civilizations of cyberpunk novels and short stories are dystopias where law and order have ceased to exist, huge corporations control the resources of the world, and hackers and crackers are the lone gunmen struggling against the governing elite.

Cyberpunk fiction is known for its cynical outlook on society and its glorification of the solitary but brilliant rebel. The Matrix movies, all strongly influenced by *Ghost in the Shell,* are perhaps the most popular manifestation of cyberpunk fiction converted into visual reality. One of the most important themes of such stories is the direct connection between human minds and computer systems.

Former *Asimov's Science Fiction* magazine editor Gardner Dozois is credited with having popularized the term "cyberpunk" as a branch of science fiction. The label was used primarily to describe the writings of William Gibson, John Shirley, Rudy Rucker, Pat Cadigan, and a number of other writers whose impact was particularly felt in the 1980s and early 1990s. William Gibson's novel *Neuromancer*, published in 1984, was perhaps the most influential of all cyberpunk works, and was surely a tremendous influence on *Ghost in the Shell*.

However, the question that we want to investigate is: what influence did *Ghost in the Shell* have on our real world? The answer is surprising.

Thermo-Optical Camouflage

The world of *Ghost in the Shell* offers a fascinating glimpse of the tomorrow-yet-to-come. Not surprisingly, though that future is still more than two decades away, a number of the prophetic elements in the show seem out of sync. Despite all of the discussion and research done on human-machine interfacing, it appears unlikely that people will be uploading their brains to computers at any time in the next quarter century. Nor do synthetic cyborg bodies seem very close, though advances in prosthetics may prove us wrong.

More to the point, the robot servants in cyborg form are nowhere near becoming reality and a society that would accept such machines seems further away than it did ten years ago. The upswing in fundamentalist religious beliefs casts a grim cloud over the future of technology and the biochemical revolution. While nanotechnology, discussed in previous chapters of this book, seems to offer unbelievable opportunities, government interference with scientific progress is on the rise, and technological breakthroughs that seem to offer the most amazing benefits to future society seem more than ever to be held hostage by the whims of politicians. In the end, we suspect it will be politics as usual that will push or pull technological advances, and the looking glass into the future seems cloudier than ever.

Still, some aspects of the future are here today. First theorized in William Gibson's *Neuromancer,* one of the most important weapons systems used by Section 9 in the *Ghost in the Shell: Stand Alone Complex* TV series is thermo-optical camouflage. This special type of body armor is worn by the members of the secret government agency as well as by their small servo-machines, known in the series as Tachikoma tanks (more about them later). This specialized armor doesn't make the people or machines invisible, but it does create optical illusions that help blend them into any environment, making them nearly invisible to the naked eye. Unfortunately, the technology is useless against radar, since the actual objects are still in place. It is a continuing stealth system, so it can be used when the operator is in motion; however, moving too swiftly while using such camouflage would most likely overload the system. Amazing as the technology is, it exists in at least rudimentary form today. And it was even showcased in a James Bond movie.

Optical camouflage is a new kind of concealment armor made possible through the use of micro-computers. It can best be called "active camouflage." The basic concept underlying the system is simple. You start with a subject such as a car or a person. Then you photograph the background behind that car or person. Finally, you project that background onto a screen in front of the subject. The object behind the screen appears to be invisible. There's nothing actually done to the object in question other than to merge it into the background. Optical camouflage is really just an updating of old camouflage techniques using digital photography and computer imaging software.

The Japanese scientist who perfected this unique form of camouflage, Dr. Sekiguchi S. Tachi, calls his invention X'tal Vision. Dr. Tachi has demonstrated X'tal Vision using what he calls a "transparent cloak." When wearing the cloak, which resembles an ordinary raincoat, a person appears to be totally transparent. Cars, trees, and people who are behind the subject can be seen clearly, thus creating the illusion that the wearer is invisible. On his Web site, Dr. Tachi does credit the original *Ghost in the Shell* anime as the main reference for X'tal Vision, perhaps the only instance in which a cartoon has been credited for inspiring an actual invention.[44]

In the James Bond movie *Die Another Day,* the same principle as the "transparent cloak" is used for an entire automobile. Thousands of tiny digital video cameras are embedded in the framework of the car. These cameras take pictures of the nearby scenery and transmit the images to projectors on the opposite side of the car. The projectors display the images as photographed by the cameras. The thousands of small images combine to form one large digital video of what is behind the car. Thus the vehicle is hidden behind a screen of scenery that blends in with the rest of the background. The image quality, of course, depends a great deal on the background scenery. If used on a busy street in Manhattan, the invisible car would most likely be a disaster, since it would project people behind the car moving in front of it. In the Bond film, the main action scenes involving the invisible car take place in an icy wilderness, so the car blends in with the environment.

What makes optical camouflage so interesting is that it is three-dimensional. Thus, a person completely covered by an optical camouflage suit would be invisible to the human eye. For the system to work smoothly, miniature cameras would have to be placed everywhere on the armor so as to photograph what is behind the object at every point. Also necessary would be screens at exactly 180-degree angles to those cameras, to maintain the illusion all the way around the object. While it would require a great deal of engineering skill, such work would not be impossible. The most important element of the armor would be the computers handling the data transfer. Information from camera to screen would have to move at near-instantaneous speeds to maintain the illusion. Radar would not be fooled by such optical camouflage, because the object being hidden is still in the same place as before. It would merely be projecting a video image of another place to the onlooker. Radar beams would still hit the projection screens and cameras of the front of the illusion and relay such information back to the operator. Thus, while optical camouflage would be useful in some spy operations, in others it would be useless.

The optical camouflage car provides some neat tricks in *Die Another Day*. But it's really just another interesting gimmick used in the movie. The camouflage technique is used to maximum advantage in *Stand Alone Complex,* but even there, it is more of a gimmick than a real spy tool. In both cases, it's science used as a source of wonder and not for any practical reason. It seems unlikely we'll be using optical camouflage clothing anytime in the near future.

The Future Is Now

The future *is* now, if we judge our modern world by some of the super science used by Section 9 in the *Ghost in the Shell* anime TV series. Along with optical camouflage, another invention that aids the police of the future is the light autonomous tank. As shown in the series, these are very lightweight tanks that stand on four legs and have two arms. They are also armed with a machine gun and a cable wire gun. When needed, they can even serve as transportation devices for Section 9 agents. In the TV series, these tanks, which are known as Tachikoma, have a limited AI program, which seems unlikely anytime in the near future. However, if we abandon the notion of AI use, Tachikoma otherwise might not be that far off. In fact, it seems fairly likely that such spider-like machines will be in use long before the events of *Ghost in the Shell* take place. Actually, somewhat stripped-down versions of the Tachikoma are already being perfected for use today, though in a somewhat different form than was envisioned by Masamune Shirow. We mentioned these machines in chapter 2; now let's examine them in more detail.

After the terrorist attack on the World Trade Center on September 11, 2001, a group of robots that could have guest-starred in the *GIS* TV series played an important role in searching for survivors in the ruins of the twin towers. These machines were dubbed "marsupial" robots by their inventors because they carry smaller robots inside them for exploring tight spaces. The experimental robots crawled through the wreckage of the twin towers searching for survivors. Dozens of robots, armed with bright lights and heat and motion detectors, were used. Some of the machines were remotely controlled, while other, smaller ones were connected to the users by cables. The robots rode on caterpillar tracks and were strong enough to push pieces of concrete out of their way.

A number of these robots came from Robin Murphy's lab at the

University of South Florida. Murphy, an associate professor at the University of South Florida (along with her research group in the Department of Computer Science and Engineering and Cognitive and Neural Sciences), is one of a small number of research scientists in the world working on designing search-and-rescue robots.

At Ground Zero, Murphy's robots were used in two basic applications. Small robots about the size of a shoe box and connected to their users by cables were used in the rubble pile for the first two weeks, when the focus still was on search and rescue. The robots' small size was made possible by the fact that they did not have to carry batteries for their power source but instead got their energy from cables. The machines were used to search spaces where survivors might still be alive. The robots also provided information as to the location of rubble for removal.

The second two weeks at Ground Zero were spent searching nearby damaged buildings. At times, city engineers cut holes in walls so the small robots could inspect the buildings from the inside. Using robots was a lot safer than having engineers probe the structures.

Murphy's larger robots are wireless and have onboard computing systems. They were used sparingly at the rescue site, but the military has high hopes for them in the not-too-distant future. These robots are designed for use by the military in urban terrain, to deal with urban terrorists and hostage situations. The onboard computing systems are designed to make the machines more intelligent and require less operator attention. Plans call for the robots to be used to navigate through buildings broadcasting what they "see" in video, while creating 3-D maps for soldiers to follow. Except for being unarmed, an oversight the army most likely will correct, these robots don't sound much different from the Tachikomas of *Ghost in the Shell*. They're another example of the present catching up with the future earlier than expected.

In one of the episodes of *Stand Alone Complex*, Section 9 borrows the Echelon wiretap system from the United States CIA. This ultimate wiretap system is shown as a pervasive communications program that monitors all telephone, wireless phone, email, and electronic data transfer in a region—in this case, Japan. The only limitation to this system is the amount of computer power and speed necessary to interpret the huge amount of data. Having written a highly praised near-future techno-thriller novel, *The Termination Node*, we are both familiar with the notorious Echelon system. There have been rumors and stories about this massive secret system floating about the Internet since the early 1990s. Most stories about Echelon don't involve the CIA but the much more secretive National Security Agency (NSA).

Since Echelon appeared in *Ghost in the Shell*, even in a minor role, we thought it would be best to investigate the latest information available on this powerful communications tool and include some of the facts about the system in this book. The more we searched, the more amazed we became. Despite well over 6,000 Web sites devoted to Echelon and similar programs designed by the government, such as Carnivore, no one seemed to have very much reliable, firsthand data on these spy systems. All of the information we found was based on supposition, suspicion, and paranoia. The so-called hard facts about the systems appeared in several books never even printed in the United States and based on less than ironclad guarantees.

Echelon may or may not exist in cyberspace today, but if it does, it's very well hidden. And it's extremely poorly used. In essence, our hunt for Echelon involved checking sources that inevitably looped us into a chain where every reference used every other reference in the circle as the source of their information. Book A thus listed Book B for its source of information. Book B listed Book C as its source of information. And, Book C listed Book A for its source. And so on and so on, in huge chains of circular logic that never progressed inward to a reliable source of information. If Echelon is trying to remain hidden, it is doing so in spectacular fashion.

We offer, with brief tidbits of commentary, what we were able to learn about Echelon, a top-secret security network used by the NSA to keep track of global communication between major criminal organizations and terrorists throughout the world.

According to *Ghost in the Shell*, Echelon exists in the year 2029. According to our 6,000 or so sources on the Internet, Echelon exists now and is watching our every move.

In the article "Somebody's Listening" by Duncan Campbell, published in the *New Statesman* for August 12, 1988, the author describes the workings of Echelon, a secret spy network established soon after the end of World War II by the United States,

Great Britain, Canada, Australia, and New Zealand. The main branch of the Echelon network was listed as located in Menwith Hill in England, cited as the largest spy installation in the world. In charge of the operation was the NSA. The Echelon operation was charged with the task of listening to all communications in the member countries and sorting out those that might hint at danger from espionage. Exactly how this immense listening and monitoring network functioned without high-speed computers was never explained.

Other work on what came to be called "signals intelligence" was done by investigative reporters such as James Bamford, who wrote a book called *The Puzzle Palace* about the billions of dollars being spent on a worldwide interception network. However, the most quoted book about the Echelon system was written by a New Zealand reporter and spy authority, Nicky Hagar, in 1996. Titled *Secret Power: New Zealand's Role in the International Spy Network,* it became the Bible of global conspiracy theorists.

According to Hagar, Echelon was a spy system designed to monitor primarily nonmilitary targets: governments, organizations, and businesses in virtually every country. The Echelon system works by indiscriminately intercepting huge amounts of communications and then siphoning out what is valuable using artificial intelligence aids like Memex to find key words.

Again, according to Hagar's self-published book, since 1981, the United States and its five allies have been tapping nearly all of the voice, fax, and email communications of its citizens.

Echelon listens in real time, from earth and space, all communications by telephone, telex, satellite communication, fax, and email. This is accomplished by secretly monitoring Intelsat satellites, which are used to convey a majority of the world's communication information. This information is filtered for words or phrases of interest to one of the member countries' intelligence services. Each country provides a "dictionary" of words and phrases, as well as a target list of organizations or persons to be monitored. Sites in the network included Sugar Grove and Yakima in the United States, Waihopai in New Zealand, Morwenstow in England, and bases in Australia and Hong Kong.

In the article "Big Brother's Watching" by Geoff Metcalf, published in *WorldNetDaily* on April 4, 1998, the author discusses the legal standing of Echelon. The network works on the principle that, while it is illegal for governments to spy on their own citizens, it is legal to have other countries in Echelon do so and then exchange information between governments. It's a minor loophole in the law, but as the article states, it's big enough for the NSA, which is known for bending the rules to achieve its goals. Worse, there are no external controls to determine who may be monitored: target requests are routinely serviced and the results delivered back to the requesting country.

While Hagar lists military intelligence as the main use for Echelon, he also quotes from a "highly placed intelligence operative" of the Intelligence Service who was interviewed by the *Observer* about misuses of the system. While most information gathered by the system concerns potential terrorists, intensive monitoring of economic intelligence of all the countries participating in the GATT negotiations also takes place. The operative also mentions that British intelligence routinely examined the phone records of Amnesty International and Christian Aid. According to the operative, the phone tap was known by the code word Mantis.

In early 2000, former Rep. Bob Barr (R-GA) convened a U.S. House of Representatives committee to investigate Echelon as well as charges that the NSA was operating far beyond its responsibilities. Barr's committee demanded the NSA turn over documents regarding Echelon, but, for the first time ever, the NSA refused, citing legal grounds. Barr's committee instead relied on the testimony of Margaret Newsham, a former NSA employee and member of the team that helped develop Echelon. Needless to say, Barr's hearing went nowhere after the events of 9/11, when the country decided that the government intelligence agencies needed greater powers, not fewer. Since that time, the FBI has been trying to gain approval for a more advanced wiretap system to be used in the United States named Carnivore. So far, attempts to put it into place and get it running have not succeeded.

It's a privacy issue that concerns all Americans, but after 9/11, most people worry more about being protected from terrorists than about whether the FBI is listening to their phone conversations. One aspect of *Ghost in the Shell* that makes it relevant to today's audiences is that Section 9 deals with cyber-terrorism.

That's a concept that has a lot of people worried. Enough so that attacks on government sites by hackers are considered major news. But is it really true?

The Cyber-Terrorism Threat

Twenty-four years from now, the dedicated police officers of *Ghost in the Shell: Stand Alone Complex* deal with cyber-criminals who threaten the very existence of Neo-Tokyo. In this series, terrorism comes in many forms—from a robot tank with a human brain to a cybernetic Robin Hood who calls himself "The Laughing Man" and who exposes the darkest secrets of corporate and industrial espionage. It's all in a day's work for the Major and her friends. The adventures are all quite exciting and seem fairly believable. Which leads us to ask: Are they? Is cyber-terrorism the crime of the future? Or is it a bill of goods we are being sold by cartoons, the mass media, and a number of huge corporations, all of whom have a vested interest in getting us concerned about cyber-crime?

Obviously, we can't know what's going to happen in the future, but we can look at statistics for cyber-crimes today and see how bad the problem is now, and how fast it is growing. The facts are surprising.

In 1996, the U. S. government carried out a series of computer attacks on itself to test its protection against online attacks. Unfortunately, 88 percent of the nearly 3,000 defense computer systems attacked were found to be "easily penetrable." Of those attacks, 96 percent were not detected. Of the approximately 100 systems in which the attacks were discovered, only 5 percent were reported to the government.[45]

A survey taken by the Science Applications International Corp. in 1996 found that forty major corporations reported losing over $800 million total to computer attacks in the past five years. An FBI survey of 428 government, corporate, and university sites found that over 40 percent reported having been broken into at least once in the last year.

Another survey found that in the 1990s, the computer systems at the Pentagon containing sensitive but unclassified information had been illegally accessed via networks 250,000 times and that only 150 of the intrusions had been detected. The FBI estimated that in 1996, U.S. businesses lost $138 million every year to hackers.

According to sources in England, terrorists collected nearly 400 million pounds from 1993 to 1995 just by threatening institutions. During that three-year period, there were forty reported threats made to banks in the United States and Britain. Some terrorists simply took the money instead of using blackmail. A Russian hacker was able to remove ten million dollars from Citibank.[46]

When asked about cyber-terrorism, Dr. Mudawi E. Mukhtar of the Computer Crime Research Center pointed out that a study covering the second half of 2002 showed that the most dangerous nation in terms of the origin of malicious cyber-attacks was the United States. In fact, 35.4 percent of all attacks came from the United States. South Korea came next, with 12.8 percent, followed by China (6.7 percent), Germany (6.2 percent) and France (4 percent). The United Kingdom came in ninth with 2.2 percent.[47]

The Computer Crime Research Center also noted that "more than half of recorded digital attacks in the past have been the result of misuse and abuse of networks by employees."[48] A recent study conducted by the Department of Homeland Security came up with similar results. The report concluded that corporate insiders who sabotage computers containing material so sensitive that they risk endangering national security or the economy are usually motivated by revenge against their bosses.[49]

The study examined dozens of computer-sabotage cases over the past six years and tried to determine what had motivated the attackers. The report described most attackers as disgruntled workers or former employees who were angry about disciplinary actions, missed promotions, or layoffs. Nearly all of the employees took some steps to conceal their identities online—sometimes even posing as coworkers—as they plotted their attacks. Attackers ranged from teens to retirees.[50]

All of this information leads us to wonder whether the danger of cyber-terrorist attacks hasn't been exaggerated by those seeking to profit from the resulting panic. It's a question that's been raised by others, not only in the United States but in England as well.

In 2002, Richard Forno, the author of *The Art of Information Warfare* and a security consultant working with the U.S. Department of Defense, attacked the British firm mi2g for spreading fear, uncertainty, and doubt about cyber-terrorism risks; he also questioned its estimates of damage caused by cyber-attacks and cyber-security "intelligence" sources.[51]

In his report, Forno raised serious questions about mi2g's estimates of the damage caused by cyber-attacks—and the basis of its "cyber-security intelligence" business generally. The main problem with mi2g, according to Forno, was the company's regular predictions of deadly cyber-terrorist attacks that never actually occurred. Forno mentions a November 11, 2002 report from mi2g that discussed the need for "counter-attack-forces" to deal with the threats of "digital mass attacks," stating that it wasn't a question of *if* such attacks would happen but *when* they would.[52] Forno's wrath was aimed in particular at a statement from the November 11, 2002 mi2g report about the costs of cyber-terrorism. According to Forno: "mi2g claimed that in November 2002 there were 57,977 'overt digital attacks' to date, and that such 'overt' attacks will cost $7.3 billion worldwide for 2002. The firm estimates that the total economic damages of all attacks—overt, covert, virus, and worms—will be between $33 and $40 billion worldwide for the year.

"It's never really clear how mi2g differentiates an 'overt' attack versus a 'covert' attack. Does a Web site defacement count as an 'overt' attack? How does one know when a 'covert' attack occurs? Isn't that what being 'covert' is all about? And how can one credibly forecast billions of dollars lost from cyber-attacks, especially from 'covert' ones the victim doesn't know have occurred?"[53]

It's worth noting that mi2g entered the computer security

scene in late 1999 by issuing a high-profile warning that the Y2K virus would cause major problems for multinational corporations. The failure of any major Y2K problems to materialize didn't help the company's reputation much, but it came back strong as a supporter of tough Internet security against terrorist groups. The 9/11 attacks sent the company's business soaring.

Despite Forno's cautious stance, there are other officials in the U.S. government who don't take the threat of cyber-terrorism lightly. Perhaps the most famous of these is Richard Clarke, special adviser for cyberspace security for the National Security Council, who served President Clinton and, later, President Bush. Clarke was fired a short time after 9/11, he says, because the president didn't want it known that he had never considered foreign terrorists a major threat to the United States. In a February 2001 interview conducted by Richard Thieme for *Information Security* magazine, Clarke claimed the president understated the potential severity of cyber-threats and that the consequences could be significant: "The economy is badly damaged, the nation is unable to operate for a period of time, and people die."[54]

One worry is that in the United States, the nation's power, water, transportation, government, and even military infrastructures rely on the Internet for communications. It doesn't take a rocket scientist to understand how a terrorist attack could cripple this infrastructure, disrupting flight patterns, for example, or causing a failure in emergency response due to power or communications loss. The events of September 11, 2001 heightened these fears and led to the creation and restructuring of multiple government agencies devoted to cyber-terrorism.

Still, many other security specialists think such fears are overblown and aimed to keep the nation on edge. These experts point out that accidents have caused the same type of widespread outages, such as the New York City electrical blackout in 2002, and the world didn't come to an end before power was restored. In June of that year at Randall's Island, New York City, a backhoe operator accidentally ripped up five 13,000-volt power cables, plunging approximately 63,000 customers into darkness. The effects of the accidental disaster caused traffic jams when traffic lights went dark. Otherwise, power was restored and the city brought back to normal within eight hours. If our infrastructure is so resilient where tangible, physical damage is concerned, would it be any less resilient where intangible, nonphysical cyber-threat is concerned?[55]

Still, people like Richard Clarke, security czar for the U.S. government, feel the United States is vulnerable and needs protection fast. Speaking at George Mason University in June 2002, Clarke stated, "Digital Pearl Harbors are happening every day; they are happening to companies all across the country."[56]

One of the greatest difficulties with cyber-terrorism is defining exactly what constitutes it. Does it make sense to compare loss of information and computer data to the loss of life at Pearl Harbor or the horrific events of September 11, 2001? Dare we compare denial of service to eBay or Yahoo! to the bombing of a federal building? Truthfully, the definition of cyber-terrorism is so unclear that it remains a catchall phrase without much real use. As such, thanks to its undefined nature, cyber-terrorism is of particular interest to politicians and businesspeople who can blame it for a multitude of sins.

With cyber-terrorism a crime that can't yet be clearly defined or defeated, how can we throw money—lots and lots of money— at the problem and hope to solve it? President Bush earmarked $50 billion dollars in the 2003 budget for "Homeland Security Information Technology." The bill was passed by Congress in Februrary 2003 and was signed into law. That's a lot of money going out to the big-name computer hardware and software manufacturers to come up with solutions to problems we can't yet define.

Is there any doubt we are fast approaching a *Ghost in the Shell* future? The only problem seems to be that we're not ready for the changes that will be here sooner than we realize.

6. Anime Evolves

The Gospel of a New Century

Before delving into the scientific principles featured in some of the best anime ever produced in Japan, it must first be made clear that, while science and mathematics do not change from country to country, history, culture, civilization, and society do.

What is considered "everyday" and "normal" in the United States is often not considered normal in Japan. Lifestyles are different, as are religious beliefs. Right-wing politicians in the United States are fond of declaring that ours is a "Christian country" and that "America was founded on Christian beliefs." While it's true that Christians form the largest religious group in the United States, that fact alone does not make it a Christian country. Nor were all of the Founding Fathers, despite some of their most dramatic rhetoric, God-fearing men. They fully understood the concept of separation of church and state and made sure that guarantees of this separation were built into the Constitution. Those facts, as we know, have not stopped politicians from linking patriotism to religion during the past two centuries.

In Japan, no politician campaigns on his or her religious beliefs. Approximately 7 percent of the country's population is Christian, and they are not known for their high-profile political aspirations. Thus, topics that combine religion and politics, such as school prayer, religious celebrations, and creation science, are not problems in the Japanese school system. Nor do these topics appear in manga; therefore, they do not appear in anime.

That doesn't mean that religion, religious beliefs, and religious philosophy aren't examined and discussed in Japanese culture. They are. And "Japanese culture," of course, includes anime. One of the most successful anime series of the past decade is *Neon Genesis Evangelion,* which in quite dramatic terms deals with Earth being invaded by semi-organic beings called Angels. We discussed this show in passing in chapter 2, but now it's time to take a look beyond its giant robots.

The series uses much Christian imagery and theology in its story line; references to creation, Adam and Eve, and Jesus Christ are present throughout. Also featured are the souls of the dead, soulless clones, angelic messengers, biomechanical robots that unite dead mothers with their children, and much more. It is highly doubtful that the original uncut and uncensored version of *Neon Genesis Evangelion* will ever play on network TV in the United States. If it did, the firestorm of criticism over the show's religious concepts would rock the halls of Congress.

The original Japanese title for the series, *Shin Seiki Evangelion*, translates as "The Gospel of the New Century." The show, written and directed by Hideaki Anno, consisted of twenty-six TV episodes that aired in 1995 and 1996. In 1997, the series was followed by two movies, *Death and Rebirth* and *End of Evangelion*. Despite the controversial nature of the series, it was originally considered to be nothing more than a typical merchandise-oriented giant robot show and was financed by two toy giants, Bandai and Sega.

The story takes place in 2015, fifteen years after an event called the "Second Impact." This disaster, supposedly caused by a meteor traveling at near light speed that smashes into Antarctica, destroys two-thirds of the world's population and tilts its axis. Now, a decade and a half later, the city of Tokyo-3 is being attacked by strange humanoid monsters called Angels. Normal weapons are useless against the Angels. The only machines capable of fighting them are biomechanical body suits, known as Evangelions. These machines are built by the mysterious organization NERV.

The focus of the series is on Shinji Ikari, one of the Evangelion pilots. Because series creator Hideaki Anno suffered from a long battle with depression before writing the series, much of the show is based on his experiences coping with depression. Thus, characters in the series are forced to deal with a wide range of mood disorders and problems with depression.

Only as the series progressed did viewers learn the mysterious truths underlying the plot. The explosion in Antarctica in 2000 wasn't actually caused by a meteor. Instead, a group of scientists discovered a being of light that they called Adam in the frozen waste. It was the first of the Angels. The being self-destructed, causing the Second Impact. Needless to say, its name, Adam, tied the being in with the Evangelions, which were also known as Evas. In Japanese, the name Eve is often translated as Eva. More important was the fact that the biomechanical Evas were inhabited by the souls of the dead mothers of the pilots who flew them. All of the pilots were born approximately nine months after the Second Impact. All thirteen Evangelions were named after an angel from the Bible. This information, along with many more references to religious, biological, and psychological concepts, was scattered throughout the series.

Another fact that only emerged after a number of episodes was that NERV, the government agency battling the Angels, was also in charge of the Human Instrumentality Project, described as a path to God man had yet not tried. The logo for NERV was "God's in His Heaven, All's Right with the World." The Human Instrumentality Project was intended to start an artificial evolution of mankind. It was claimed that the event would bring about the salvation of mankind with the creation of a new Earth.

SEELE, a branch of NERV, was the group behind this project. According to the leaders of SEELE, mankind had to evolve or it would die off. SEELE proposed a forced evolution that would merge all human souls into one and put an end to all pain. It should be mentioned that *Seele* is the German word for "soul" while *Nerv* is the German word for "nerve."

When *Neon Genesis Evangelion* was first broadcast in Japan, it ran during a time slot aimed at teenagers. It was not a hit. However, when it was run a second time in a later time slot, when adults could watch it, the series became quite popular. When the series concluded, Hideaki Anno received a number of death threats from fans who felt the last two episodes had ruined the series. That's why, in 1997, he directed *The End of Evangelion*, which was released as a feature film. The movie, which was as ambiguous as the last two episodes of the TV series, did quite well as a feature film but didn't really satisfy anyone who wanted a clear explanation of how the story concluded. Fans and critics of the series have debated ever since exactly what ending Anno originally planned for the series—the TV version or the somewhat different movie version.

Neon Genesis Evangelion is one of the most popular and influential animes ever produced. Yet, despite its unusual use of Christian imagery, convoluted plot line, and morally indeterminate conclusion, the most controversial theme in the series is its underlying scientific belief in evolution. According to the plot of *Neon Genesis Evangelion,* humankind has undergone startling changes over the millennia through evolution, and the next step in the evolutionary chain is almost here. It's a theme, strangely enough, that also serves as the basis for perhaps the most famous anime film ever produced—a movie titled *Akira,* which we will discuss next.

Who Is Akira?

The original manga *Akira,* by writer/artist Katsuhiro Otomo, began publication in December 1982 in Japan's *Young Magazine* and finally concluded in July 1990. The collected manga totaled more than 2,100 pages of story and was released in six collected volumes by Kodansha. In 1988, the manga was reprinted for the first time in the United States by Epic Comics. This colorized English version concluded in 1995. An English version of the six-volume collection was released in the United States in 2000 by Dark Horse Comics.

The film version of *Akira* was written, directed, designed, and supervised by Katsuhiro Otomo during a two-year break from 1986

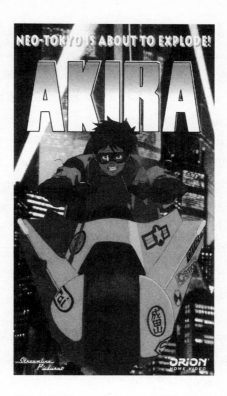

to 1988. Most of the character designs and basic settings were bor-
rowed from the manga, but the plot was somewhat different than
the comic due at least in part to the length of the film and its budget.

In 1988, the film version of *Akira* defined the cutting edge
of anime around the world. *Akira* is often described as the
movie that created a mass audience for Japanese animation in
the United States. At the time of its production, *Akira* was the
most ambitious anime movie ever made; it cost more than $12
million to produce. It did not do particularly well in Japan and

THE SCIENCE OF ANIME

was considered a flop for several years. However, the movie was a hit overseas and helped introduce anime into many foreign markets. The tagline for *Akira,* "Neo-Tokyo is about to explode!" remains one of the most famous catchphrases ever invented for an animated feature.

One of the most important points about *Akira*—which is often lost in discussions of the film—is its name. Akira, which sounds somewhat mystical and strange in English, is a common name in Japan. It's mostly a boy's name, but there are girls named Akira as well. Perhaps the most famous Akira known to Western film fans is Akira Kurosawa, the director of *Yojimbo* and *The Seven Samurai.* In Japan, naming a book or movie *Akira* is akin to titling it *Jack* in the United States.

For all its complexity, *Akira* starts out simply enough. The story begins in Neo-Tokyo, a city rebuilt over Tokyo Bay thirty years after it was destroyed (at the beginning of World War III). A gang of young bikers led by a tough but smart teenager named Kaneda is involved in a fast-paced motorcycle duel with another motorcycle gang on the streets of the big city. Meanwhile, a man holding what appears to be a 100-year-old child tries to elude the police. The man is shot, and the child, Takashi, screams. The scream smashes all the buildings around him. In the resulting confusion, the child escapes. Two of the man's friends, Kay and Ryu, are watching. The Colonel, a mysterious authority figure working for the state, takes Masaru, another strange-looking child, to find Takashi.

Tying the two threads together, Tetsuo, another biker, almost runs down Takashi. Tetsuo's bike explodes. Before anyone can react, a group of government agents grabs both Tetsuo and the child and disappears with them. The rest of Kaneda's gang is arrested. While being processed, Kaneda meets Kay and talks to her. Neither of them know that Tetsuo is being studied by army doctors. They discover that he has latent psi powers and the Colonel orders that Tetsuo be kept as a prisoner and taught to use his powers. Tetsuo escapes from the army, but in a fit of rage, he almost kills a rival biker before Kaneda stops him. Tetsuo's temper nearly overwhelms him before he's recaptured by the army.

Tetsuo is held in the hospital, where he has terrible nightmares. Meanwhile, another of the very strange children meets with the Colonel. Her name is Kyoko, and she tells the Colonel she had a dream in which Akira awoke. Worried, the Colonel goes to see Akira, a young boy frozen at 5 degrees above absolute zero.

Meanwhile, Ryu and Kay plan to break into the hospital to free another one of the strange children. Kaneda becomes involved in their plans. It turns out that Ryu is working for a member of the ruling council of the city. This council, a bunch of corrupt politicians, is unhappy with the Colonel's Akira Project. It has been running for years with no results. The Colonel warns the council that if they cut his funding, he will not be responsible for the consequences.

After that, events start happening fast. Kaneda travels with Ryu and Kay to the hospital hoping to rescue Tetsuo. Tetsuo's head starts throbbing in pain: the other children in the hospital are trying to force him to use his psychic powers. Tetsuo fights a psychic duel with Takashi and Masaru. The Colonel arrives and stops the fight. Tetsuo's head feels worse and worse. Tetsuo learns that Akira, one of the other children, had the same problem years before. Tetsuo angrily demands to know where Akira is, but no one will tell him. That's when Kaneda arrives to rescue Tetsuo. But all Tetsuo wants is his head fixed. He learns that Akira is located beneath the new Olympic Stadium and teleports himself out of the hospital.

An angry Tetsuo makes his way back to the bar where Kaneda's gang hangs out. He takes every drug in the place, but nothing helps with the pain, so he kills the bartender. He also kills one of his fellow gang members. Tetsuo has grown mentally unstable. Kaneda knows that he has to stop Tetsuo before he does anything worse.

Tetsuo goes to the Olympic Stadium, destroying everything he comes into contact with. Beneath the stadium is Akira's cryogenic chamber. Tetsuo is confronted there by Kay. She is being mentally controlled by the three remaining children. They tell Tetsuo that they must never use their full psychic powers or it will cause a catastrophe. A fight takes place and Tetsuo wins. He discovers that the only thing left of Akira is some containers with a print of his nervous system.

A huge battle takes place in the Olympic Stadium between Tetsuo and just about everyone else. The three children appear and beg for Akira's help. The containers burst open and Akira reappears. It was his incredible power that destroyed Tokyo thirty-eight years ago. Using that same power, he destroys Tetsuo. The remaining children sacrifice themselves to save Kaneda's life. When the explosions finally end, he rides off with his friends.

While the basic story line of *Akira* is compelling, on close examination, it doesn't make a lot of sense. How did the blast of psychic energy from Akira that destroyed Tokyo in the past start World War III? What did the city council hope to accomplish by using the remaining three children? These and other questions are never answered (or even addressed) in *Akira*. The story moves fast enough that points of logic can be ignored. Still, once again, the basic underlying theme of the film is one that might cause some school board members in conservative districts of the United States to insist the video carry a warning tag on its cover: "This movie promotes the theory of evolution. This theory has not been proven to be true."

Evolution Under Attack

Both *Akira* and *Neon Genesis Evangelion* are based on the biological principle that man is a living organism and, as such, is growing and changing over time. This process of continual change is known as evolution. Usually, these changes take place over a number of generations. The changes are a result of a process known as natural selection, which acts on the genetic variation among individual members of a species and results in a better or more complex organism.

Put another way, evolution is the process in which a living species changes for the better over a long period of time. These changes are often, though not always, caused by changes in the organism's environment. Mutations take place among the general population. Those mutations that can best help the species survive are the ones that are passed on to future generations. That simple but logical process is known as natural selection, which is often called "survival of the fittest."

The theory of evolution as stated by Charles Darwin is as much theory as is the theory of gravity or the theory of relativity. However, unlike theories of physics, the theory of evolution has been hotly debated in America for the past eighty years, beginning with the infamous Scopes "Monkey" trial in 1925. And it is still argued today, while the rest of the industrialized world watches and wonders exactly what's wrong with science in the United States. They know that evolution is the theory that binds together all biological research. It is one of the unifying themes of modern science. They understand that evolution can be both a fact and a theory and wonder why we don't understand it.

Akira and *Neon Genesis Evangelion* are pro-evolution shows— as are all anime and cartoon adventures that feature mutant humans or humans who evolve into some nonhuman state. A vast majority of people who do not believe in evolution believe that the Bible is literally true. They believe that man was created by God approximately six thousand years ago, as were all animals and plants on Earth. Since evolution takes hundreds of thousands, if not millions of years, to work, they do not accept it. Besides, assuming that God created man "in his own image," to believe that humans can evolve in new and different ways is to believe that humans can be made better than God, which is unacceptable to religious belief.

People who believe that God created the world in six days (he rested on the seventh) some six thousand years ago are called "creationists." A vast majority of creationists are Evangelical Christians. In a recent poll, 86 percent of Evangelicals felt that creationism should be taught in public schools.[57] The same group also thought that Christianity should be made the U.S. national religion.[58]

For the past several decades, creationists have been challenging the right of public schools to teach evolution in the classroom. The argument most often used by anti-evolutionists is that Darwin's theory of evolution is exactly what it says it is—a theory. And theories are not facts. Unless, as mentioned above, they are.

When creationists talk about biological evolution, they often blur the line between the questions "Does evolution take place?" and "How does evolution work?" The answer to the first question is already known. Biologists are certain beyond a shadow of a doubt that evolution takes place. The amount of evidence that it has happened and is still happening is overwhelming. The answer to the second question is still being determined. There are several theories about the exact mechanism of evolution. So what? No one questions the fact that gravity works, even though we are still not sure, after thousands of years of research, exactly how. The great scientist Stephen J. Gould put it best:

> Well, evolution is a theory. It is also a fact. And facts and theories are different things, not rungs in a hierarchy of increasing certainty. Facts are the world's data. Theories are structures of ideas that explain and interpret facts. Facts don't go away when scientists debate rival theories to explain them. Einstein's theory of gravitation replaced Newton's in this century, but apples didn't suspend themselves in midair, pending the outcome. And humans evolved from ape-like ancestors whether they did so by Darwin's proposed mechanism or by some other yet to be discovered.
>
> Moreover, "fact" doesn't mean "absolute certainty"; there ain't no such animal in an exciting and complex world. The final proofs of logic and mathematics flow deductively from stated premises and achieve certainty only because they are not about the empirical world. Evolutionists make no claim for perpetual truth, though creationists often do (and then attack us falsely for a style of argument that they themselves favor). In science "fact" can only mean "confirmed to such a degree that it would be perverse to withhold provisional consent." I suppose that apples might start to rise tomorrow, but

the possibility does not merit equal time in physics classrooms.[59]

In the early 1980s, with the huge growth of the Evangelical movement, it seemed inevitable that creationism would someday be taught in public schools. But, many Americans who believed in many of the tenets of the Bible didn't want material they considered strictly religious in nature being taught as science in classrooms. Creationism proponents therefore tried to reinvent their beliefs as "creation science," but with no real science to back up what were statements of faith, the creationist movement faltered. Until, that is, it found a new way of reinventing itself as a new science movement, called Intelligent Design. ID, as it is usually called, argues that the universe is such a complex place that some processes and actions could not happen entirely by chance; that the development of life on Earth is so complex that the only way life could have appeared on the planet was through the efforts of a being directing the processes that lead to life. In other words, the world was designed by some being (perhaps God) who handled all the detail work that would not have happened only through natural processes.

In the 1980s Phillip E. Johnson started studying evolution. He decided that the evidence supporting evolution was very thin. Johnson also didn't believe that God created the world in six days. These beliefs inspired him to write the book *Darwin on Trial,* which was the beginning of the Intelligent Design movement.

After several years of arguing that Intelligent Design was not merely creationism in scientific clothing, the ID movement got a tremendous boost with the publication of *Darwin's Black Box* by biochemist Michael Behe in 1996. Behe invented the term "irreducible complexity." According to Behe, evolutionary actions cannot explain the emergence of certain complex biochemical cellular systems. He argued that the systems therefore must have been deliberately designed by some intelligent being. He never names the being, but most ID supporters make it clear they think this all-powerful designer is God. Behe's arguments collapse when the nature of the intelligent designer is discussed. Since the ID designer must be of irreducible complexity and therefore cannot have been created by natural processes, then it must be God. And once ID settles on God as the designer, the entire argument slips back into creationism.

Numerous scientists and scientific organizations have recognized Intelligent Design as another method of trying to teach biblical ideas in science classes. There have been hundreds of articles written refuting every ID claim. Perhaps one of the best appeared in the July 2002 *Scientific American*. Titled "15 Answers to Creationist Nonsense" by John Rennie, the article slashed every major creationist and Intelligent Design theory to shreds. And then crushed those shreds to dust.[60]

We end this short discussion of creationism and its evil twin, ID, with some remarks from John Rennie's strong argument from *Scientific American:*

Intelligent design offers few answers. For instance, when and how did a designing intelligence intervene in life's history? By creating the first DNA? The first cell? The first human? Was every species designed, or just a few early ones? Proponents of intelligent-design theory frequently decline to be pinned down on these points. They do not even make real attempts to reconcile their disparate ideas about intelligent design. Instead they pursue argument by exclusion—that is, they belittle evolutionary explanations as farfetched or incomplete and then imply that only design-based alternatives remain.

Logically, this is misleading: even if one naturalistic explanation is flawed, it does not mean that all are. Moreover, it does not make one intelligent-design theory more reasonable than another. Listeners are essentially left to fill in the blanks for themselves, and some will undoubtedly do so by substituting their religious beliefs for scientific ideas.

Time and again, science has shown that methodological naturalism can push back ignorance, finding increasingly detailed and informative answers to mysteries that once seemed impenetrable: the nature of light, the causes of disease, how the brain works. Evolution is doing the same with the riddle of how the living world took shape. Creationism, by any name, adds nothing of intellectual value to the effort.[61]

The Next Step in Human Evolution

As far as this book is concerned, evolution is a fact of life. Life on Earth began approximately 3 billion years ago. Over the course of that time, life developed from a single-celled organism into thousands upon thousands of plants and animals, the foremost of which (at least in our opinion) is humankind.

If we take a more cosmic approach to humanity, we note that Earth itself is somewhere around 4.5 billion years old and is expected, unless we do something really stupid, to last another 4 to 5 billion years. According to most scientists, humankind evolved as a separate and distinct species approximately 100,000 years ago. Some scientists feel that humans actually didn't develop until 50,000 years ago, but, as we'll soon show, cutting the years in half or doubling them doesn't really matter.

Let's make the assumption that life started 3 billion years ago. We will also assume that the life span of Earth, from beginning to end, is 10 billion years (give or take 500 million years in either direction). Such numbers are incomprehensible to the human mind, so why don't we think of the life of Earth as taking place over the course of one day. Let's call it our cosmic day. Using that as a reference point, we can say pretty accurately that life on Earth has been around for seven hours and twelve minutes of the cosmic day. Which is a fairly good amount of time considering that Earth is still less than half the day old. Humankind, however, has been around for less than half a second, and civilization (say the past 5,000 years) has lasted for less than a fiftieth of a second on the cosmic scale.

Just in case we need another reminder of how insignificant we are in the lifetime of the planet, much less the universe, let's recall for an instant the dinosaurs. Big and stupid, dinosaurs had brains the size of peas. For all their stupidity, dinosaurs managed to survive three periods of Earth's history—the Triassic, Cretaceous, and Jurassic ages. In total, dinosaurs existed for 165 million years. In the grand scheme of things, dinosaurs lived for just under 24 minutes of our 24-hour cosmic day. The average lifetime of a species on Earth is a few million years. Every year, often with our help, thousands of species cease to exist. Ozymandias, anybody?

What then of humanity? The underlying theme of both *Akira* and *Neon Genesis Evangelion* is that humankind has stopped evolving and that some artificial stimulus is needed to start the process again. It's interesting to note that in both animes, that jump-start mechanism involves some sort of immense explosion killing millions of people. Another striking similarity between the movie and the TV show is that the military (or a paramilitary organization) is behind the "forced" evolution, and that meddling is not only secretive but deadly. One of the basic beliefs in nearly all science fiction anime is that the military cannot be trusted. Still, in *Akira* and *Neon Genesis Evangelion*, the military is trying to help humanity move forward.

Are the colonels and generals right? Has humanity stopped

evolving? Very few scientists think so. But not for the reasons you might think.

Ian Pearson, in his article "The Future of Human Evolution," argues that Darwinian evolution no longer applies to mankind: "Homo sapiens' control of the environment, and mobility around it," he writes, "has already removed one key mechanism—local isolation—that was believed to drive speciation and thus evolution. Homo sapiens may have limited his natural evolutionary ability by his very success at exploiting a wide range of ecological niches."[62]

Pearson contends that Darwinian evolution doesn't matter to humankind, as genetic engineering and man-machine interfaces have made the concept of survival of the fittest obsolete. A number of other scientists hold the same belief: that humankind is no longer controlled by evolution but is controlling evolution.

Another author who believes that humanity has already moved beyond Darwin and is about to take a gigantic evolutionary step forward is Joel Garreau. Joel is a senior writer for the *Washington Post* in Washington, D.C., president of his company, The Garreau Group, and a member of the scenario-planning consortium Global Business Network. His new and quite controversial book, published in 2005, is titled *Radical Evolution*.

According to Garreau, humanity is heading for a flash-point breakdown of humankind into three distinct subspecies. He calls the first type "enhanced humans." These are the people who have the money and enthusiasm necessary to make themselves live longer, think smarter, and look sexier. The second kind of humans would be the "naturals," those people who would sneer at enhancements, and, while they could afford all sorts of biological upgrades, refuse to get them. Snobs of the evolutionary tree, so to speak. The third group would consist of everyone else: all the people who might want to be enhanced but aren't sure about it, but who won't ever find out because they don't have the money to pay for the improvements anyway. If we project Garreau's dream a few hundred thousand years into the future and throw in some natural catastrophes, we find ourselves faced with H. G. Wells's nightmare world of *The Time Machine,* complete with ruthless Morlocks living beneath the ground and innocent Eloi living aboveground.

Want to see Garreau's enhanced humans right now? Take a look at Barry Bonds and other sports superstars accused of taking steroids. Think of a half-dozen of Hollywood's most beautiful movie stars, who've had breast implants, plastic surgery, and botox injections to change their appearances. And who work out every day with their own personal trainer, eat meals prepared by the cook and dietician, and who change the color of their hair, skin, and eyes with the same concern with which most of us change our clothes.

Another researcher studying future evolution is Peter Ward of the University of Washington, whose book *Future Evolution* puts a grim face on what will come in the next few centuries. Ward feels that humankind is making itself extinction-proof by

THE SCIENCE OF ANIME

modifying the plants and animals that still exist in our world to our norms. We've eliminated the survival of the fittest part of Darwin's theory by eliminating anything that might threaten our survival. The only thing that might threaten humanity's survival is an accidental plague virus or unknown highly lethal epidemic caused by our own tampering with the genetic cord. Ward sees a human settlement on Mars as an answer to this possible future. A colony on another planet would insure the future of humankind, as even the total destruction of all life on Earth would not put an end to our species.

In "The Future of Human Evolution," Ian Pearson offers the most controversial evolutionary path for mankind, one that doesn't please everyone. But there's no doubt that many of the facts he quotes are true, and history has a way of rushing far ahead of any prediction. Pearson sees our world as becoming the home planet for a bunch of super-scientific man-machine cyborgs, controlling powers we can hardly imagine. Here is Pearson's projection for the way human evolution will progress over the next several hundred years:

Robotus primus

For a time at least, according to Pearson, humankind will be the second-smartest beings on Earth. Computers will most likely surpass our intelligence in around 2015. It won't be until years later that they develop the technology to raise us to their level. Pearson calls these super robots Robotus primus.

Homo cyberneticus

Already, scientists have developed silicon chips that interface with human nerve cells in various cybernetic prostheses. Other extensions to the body are in development. Some people claim that thoughts can be recognized and detected without any physical contact. Assuming telepathy exists, it seems reasonable to expect that computers will be developed that can interface directly with humans. This is the underlying theme of *Ghost in the Shell* and its sequels. Soon after this interface takes place, technology will produce a total mind-link between man and machine. That's when humans will be able to enhance our mental ability by using external processing as an adjunct to our own brains. Since by this time the machines will be smarter than us, this will be a large step forward for humankind. This new species will be called Homo cyberneticus. Pearson suspects many humans will not be able to accept such changes and will slowly but surely die out.

Homo hybridus

The final type of new human would be those who accept cybernetic enhancement and use genetic enhancement to redesign their bodies and those of their descendents. It is likely that many of the people who accept cybernetic enhancement would lend themselves to genetic enhancement, too, or would allow enhancement of their offspring. As best imagined, these beings—with cybernetic attachments and genetically altered bodies—would be the ultimate humans. Or at least Pearson believes so.

Neon Genesis Evangelion and *Akira* see rapid genetic change brought about by mutation due to society's pressures. In later episodes of *Gundam Wing,* similar events take place when a new race of genetic warriors, Newtypes, start causing trouble. Another series, *E's Otherwise,* features mutated humans who have mastered the power of changing thoughts into energy. Evolution in anime is seen as a haphazard and dangerous method of advancing the human spirit. Yet many shows feature genetically altered warriors and secret agents equipped with man-machine interfaces. Change is coming to humanity, and this has been well predicted in anime. The interesting question, though, is which anime's predictions are correct?

Does it really matter? We might not have a voice at all in what we look like. Or in whether or not we even survive. Here we refer to that classic but still contemporary tale of our world and a dire danger we continue to ignore. The anime is named *Nausicaa of the Valley of the Wind,* and its view of the future of Earth is not one most visitors find appealing.

Nausicaa of the Valley of the Wind

One of the most popular anime movies ever produced, *Nausicaa of the Valley of the Wind* was the first major film written and directed by Hayao Miyazaki. As mentioned earlier in this book, Miyazaki began his career in the children's manga field in the 1960s. In 1982 he began writing *Nausicaa* for *Animage,* an animation-fan magazine. The story proved so popular that Tokuma, one of Japan's largest publishers, financed a feature-length animated film based on the manga directed by Miyazaki. The movie followed (with some minor changes) the story of the first two volumes of the manga. Miyazaki continued writing the manga after the film was released and finally finished it in 1994.

Nausicaa was a huge hit, and its popularity led Tokuma to finance a new animation company, Studio Ghibli, which primarily produced animated features based on Miyazaki's work and on that of a fellow artist, Isao Takahata. In the past few years, Disney has been releasing Miyazaki's work in the United States in limited theatrical release and on DVDs.

Nausicaa of the Valley of the Wind takes place thousands of years in the future after a war and the ensuing ecological holocaust has destroyed much of the world and wiped out nearly all of humankind. According to legends, the destruction took place during the Seven Days of Fire, when genetic monsters described as God Warriors engaged in a terrible battle. Now, many centuries later, humanity exists only in small settlements and kingdoms on

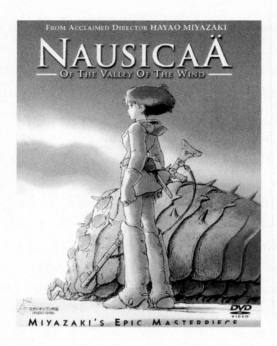

the edge of what is called the Sea of Corruption, a huge fungus forest filled with poisonous plants that covers a vast majority of the land on Earth. Living in these forests are the Ohmu, a race of giant insect creatures who are not affected by the poison gas released by the glowing fungus. The inhabitants of these towns fight a constant battle to keep the giant fungus from engulfing their small farms. In this post-holocaust world—right out of *Mad Max*—a vast majority of modern technology has been lost or forgotten. A few machines still exist, such as airplanes and tanks, but these are the last remaining examples of their type, dug up from the ruins of ancient cities and war bases.[63]

The Valley of the Wind is a tiny coastal kingdom where the winds from the sea provide power via windmills. Nausicaa is princess of this kingdom, though she seems to have no major responsibilities and her position appears to be mostly ceremonial. Nausicaa is also an expert pilot who flies about on her jet-powered glider. Wearing a gas mask, she studies the poisonous plants and giant insects that live in the Sea of Corruption.

Soon after we are introduced to Nausicaa and the other inhabitants of the Valley of the Wind, the village is overrun by the army of the Empire of Talmechia. Realizing that they stand no chance against the Talmechian army, with its tanks and airplanes, the people of the Valley of the Wind surrender without a fight. Little do they know that the Talmechia leader has come to the Valley of the Wind for a purpose other than conquest.

In fact, the invaders plan to resurrect one of the ancient God Warriors and use it to burn away the Sea of Corruption. Needless to say, Nausicaa and several of her friends believe that bringing one of the God Warriors, who destroyed the world, back to life is a bad idea. Things go from bad to worse when the reanimated Warrior collapses before fulfilling his new mission, and the Ohmu advance on the Valley of the Wind. Fortunately, Nausicaa figures out the truth about the ecology of the poisoned Earth and manages to save her loyal subjects just in the nick of time.

According to an interview with Miyazaki, Nausicaa is named after a princess who appears in *The Odyssey*. He combined her with a legendary Japanese princess called The Princess Who

Loved Bugs (because she loved playing in the fields and watching insects).[64] Nausicaa is not the first children's character or animated figure to warn about the dangers of redesigning the atmosphere and biosphere of the world. Many villains have expressed the desire to wipe Earth clean of people in order to start life on the planet all over with the villain him- or herself playing God. Several of the best James Bond villains planned such schemes—only to be defeated, just in the nick of time, by Bond and his usual beautiful but deadly associate.

The biggest surprise of the *Nausicaa* manga and movie is that it became popular in Japan, a country not known for its protection of the environment. The Japanese population largely ignored environmental issues during the 1950s and 1960s, despite worsening environmental problems, while the government instead concentrated on economic growth. By the end of the 1960s, citizens' groups, local governments, courts, and the media were forcing environmental problems—particularly those involving pollution—onto the national agenda. Environmental policy in Japan reflects a process in which pressure was either built from the bottom up or came from outside Japan, rather than being exerted from the top down. While some major problems were addressed, others were not.

The 1989 United Nations Environment Programme survey showed that Japan had the lowest level of concern for and awareness of environmental issues among policy makers and the public out of fourteen countries surveyed. Japan also had the lowest percentage of people believing that they should contribute time and money to environmental groups.[65]

Japan, as a country, wasn't ready for global conservation reform in the 1980s, though *Nausicaa of the Valley of the Wind* was a good first step. As were the warnings presented by James Lovelock in his controversial book *Gaia: A New Look at Life on Earth*, which was published around the world in 1979. In his Gaia theory, Lovelock warned that if humans did not take better care of our home planet, that planet might rise up and take care of humans once and for all. While Gaia theory is one of the most controversial evolutionary theories presented in the past century, it's also one of the most discussed and debated. Meaning that someday, it might actually save the world. As it did in *Nausicaa*.

Gaia

Back in the 1960s, Dr. James Lovelock was not part of a university, research institute, or business firm. He was not a wealthy man. But he was the British scientist who invented the electron capture detector, a device that found the widespread residues of pesticides throughout the world. It was his device that led to the publication of Rachel Carson's 1962 book *Silent Spring*. That's the book most historians and scientists believe launched the modern environmental movement. More recently, Lovelock's invention has been used to chart the global distribution of chlorofluorocarbons and nitrous oxide, two compounds that are linked with the destruction of the ozone layer in our atmosphere.

Lovelock's genius was recognized by NASA in the 1970s, when he was invited to be part of the Viking team investigating the existence of life on Mars. Lovelock's job was to design instruments that could be sent on a spacecraft to Mars and that were capable of detecting the presence of life there. This wasn't an easy mission, since it was hard to know what to test for: any life forms on Mars would be radically different from those on Earth.

The job led him to think about what actually constitutes life, and how it can be detected. He decided that the most general characteristic of life is that it takes in energy and matter and discards waste products. He also reasoned that other kinds of organism would use the planet's atmosphere as the medium for this cyclic exchange, just as we breathe in oxygen and expel carbon dioxide. He speculated that life would therefore leave a detectable chemical signature on the Martian atmosphere. Maybe it could be detected from Earth, so it wouldn't even be necessary to send a spaceship to Mars.

To test this idea, Lovelock and a colleague, Dian Hitchcock, analyzed the chemical makeup of Mars, and compared it with that of Earth. The results showed a strong contrast. The atmosphere of Mars, like Venus, was about 95 percent carbon dioxide, with some oxygen and no methane. The Earth is 77 percent nitrogen, 21 percent oxygen, and a relatively large amount of methane. From this information, Lovelock reasoned that Mars was chemically dead; all the reactions that were going to take place had already done so. Earth, however, is far from chemical equilibrium. For example, methane and oxygen will react with each other very easily, and yet both are present in the atmosphere. Lovelock concluded that for this to be the case, the gases must be in constant circulation—and that the pump driving this circulation was life.[66]

Lovelock decided to study the history of life's interaction with the atmosphere. He noted that about three billion years ago, bacteria and photosynthetic algae started to remove carbon dioxide from the atmosphere, producing oxygen as a waste product. Over enormous time periods, this process changed the chemical content of the atmosphere—to the point where organisms began to suffer from oxygen poisoning! The situation was only relieved with the advent of organisms powered by aerobic consumption.

It was life processes, the cumulative actions of countless organisms, he realized, that controlled the atmosphere. If viewed from outer space, the mass effect of these processes was that Earth itself appeared as a living entity—especially in comparison with its dead neighbors. Lovelock came to the understanding that Earth could best be described as a kind of super-organism. Years later, Lovelock stated: "For me, the personal revelation of Gaia came quite suddenly—like a flash of enlightenment. I was in a small room on the top floor of a building at the Jet Propulsion Laboratory in Pasadena, California. It was the autumn of 1965 . . . and I was talking with a colleague, Dian Hitchcock, about a paper we were preparing. . . . It was at that moment that I glimpsed Gaia. An awesome thought came to me. The Earth's atmosphere was an extraordinary and unstable mixture of gases, yet I knew that it was constant in composition over quite long periods of time. Could it be that life on Earth not only made the atmosphere, but also regulated it—keeping it at a constant composition, and at a level favorable for organisms?"[67]

On a walk with his neighbor, the novelist William Golding, Lovelock described his theory and asked for advice on a name. Golding suggested Gaia, after the Greek goddess of Earth. The Gaia Hypothesis was born.

In 1979, Lovelock wrote the book *Gaia: A New Look at Life on Earth*, which developed his ideas. He stated in the book that ". . . the physical and chemical condition of the surface of Earth, of the atmosphere, and of the oceans has been and is actively made fit and comfortable by the presence of life itself. This is in contrast to the conventional wisdom, which held that life adapted to the planetary conditions as it and they evolved their separate ways."[68]

The main concept behind Lovelock's work was his assertion that Earth is self-regulating. He knew that the heat of the sun has increased by 25 percent since life began on Earth, yet Earth's temperature has remained more or less constant. However, he didn't know exactly what mechanisms were behind the regulation. It wasn't until he began collaborating with the American microbiologist Lynn Margulis that the full Gaia theory began to take shape. Margulis was studying the processes by which living organisms produce and remove gases from the atmosphere. In particular, she was examining the role of microbes that live in Earth's soil.

Working together, the two scientists uncovered a number of feedback loops that act as regulatory influences.

One example is the carbon dioxide cycle. Volcanoes constantly produce huge amounts of carbon dioxide. Since carbon dioxide is a greenhouse gas, it tends to warm Earth. If not regulated, it would make Earth too warm to support life. While plants and animals take in and expel carbon dioxide through life processes such as photosynthesis, respiration, and decay, these processes remain in balance and don't affect the net amount of the gas. Which means there has to be another process that regulates the carbon dioxide.

The other process by which carbon dioxide is removed from the atmosphere is rock weathering, wherein rainwater and carbon dioxide combine with rocks to form carbonates. Lovelock, Margulis, and others discovered that the process was greatly accelerated by the presence of bacteria in the soil. The carbonates are washed away into the ocean, where microscopic algae use them to make tiny shells. When the algae die, their shells sink to the bottom of the ocean, forming limestone sediments. Limestone is so heavy that it gradually sinks beneath Earth's mantle, where it melts. Eventually, some of the carbon dioxide contained in the limestone is fed back into the atmosphere through another volcano.

Since the soil bacteria are more active in high temperatures, the removal of carbon dioxide is accelerated when the planet is hot. This has the effect of cooling the planet. Therefore the whole massive cycle forms a feedback loop.[69]

Lovelock and Margulis identified a number of other feedback loops that operate in a similar way. An interesting feature of these loops is that, like the carbon dioxide cycle, they often combine living and nonliving components.

The Gaia Hypothesis stirred up a lot of interest and controversy when it was first presented. Many scientists found the notion of Earth acting much like a living organism fascinating. Others were not so easily convinced. The Gaia Hypothesis attracted a great deal of criticism. Lovelock had emphasized in his work that Earth seemed to regulate itself. Other scientists felt that this meant that Earth was acting as a living organism. In response to his critics, Lovelock stated the following: "Whether right or wrong, Gaia provides a very different, a top-down view, of our planet, in a world where science grows ever more conservative and dogmatic. I think we need to make room for the kinds of errors that lead us closer to the truth."[70]

Still, mere words would not satisfy those scientists who were convinced Gaia was an absolutely insane idea. So, Lovelock, working with Andrew Watson, came up with Daisyworld, an entirely imaginary planet that survives simply by following its natural processes.

"Imagine," said Lovelock, "a planet just like Earth, and orbiting a star just like the sun. This imaginary planet has a surface of bare earth, but is well watered and capable of supporting plant growth. It is seeded with daisies of two different colors, one dark and the other light. The star that warms Daisyworld is like our own sun, one that warms up as it grows older. The object of the model is to show that the simple growth and competition for space between the two daisy species can keep the temperature of Daisyworld constant and comfortable over a wide range of radiant heat output from the star."[71]

The Daisyworld planet contains of only two species of life: light daisies and dark daisies. Light daisies tend to reflect light, which has a cooling effect, while dark ones absorb radiation, and therefore warm the planet. Growth of the daisies depends on the present population, the natural death rate, the available space, and the temperature. The planet revolves around a sun, from which it absorbs energy at a rate that depends on the sun's luminosity and the albedo of the planet. It also radiates heat out to the universe, at a rate determined by the Stefan-Boltzmann law.

Interestingly, when the model is run with the sun's luminosity gradually increasing, the populations of the light and dark daisies adjust themselves naturally so as to keep the temperature constant at the optimal level for daisy growth. Daisyworld is an example of a self-regulating system. Feedback loops between the daisies and the planet temperature, contained in the equations relating growth rate to albedo, somehow conspire to maintain the conditions suitable for life.[72]

Daisyworld demonstrates the principle of self-regulation very convincingly. It's a viable ecosystem that regulates its temperature without any recourse to selection or teleology.

One of the main ideas to have come out of the Daisyworld model is that the species in an ecosystem can be concerned with nothing more than their own survival, yet as a consequence of their actions help not only themselves but the whole system. We could say that the self-regulation is an emergent property of the system. There isn't any need for the light and dark daisies to get together and agree on quotas for each other's populations, and fix growth rates and argue over how much land should be left uncovered. They just do their own thing, and the planet takes care of itself. All that is necessary is that the daisies give positive and negative feedback to the temperature, and since they are happiest at a particular temperature, they tend to keep the planet at around that temperature. They make the planet suit them.[73]

Gaia theory has had a huge impact on science, and has changed the way we view our place in the world. By making us more aware of the damage we are doing to the eco-system, it may also help us to survive. From Daisyworld, we've learned that damage once done to a planet is very difficult to undo. Our foolish meddling with global warming cannot be halted when we're uncomfortable with the effects; by then it could be too late. And once a species is extinct, it cannot be restored. We're merely one part of a large system, and we depend on that system for our survival. Damaging it damages us.

7. **Parallel Universes**

Worlds Near and Far

Fantasy anime worlds in Japan aren't just wild swords-and-sorcery adventures. Rather, logic and intelligence are used to create worlds that are a mixture of science and fantasy. Some of these anime worlds are so popular that they attract fans of both science and fantasy, and they cover science topics that are interesting to readers looking for scientific principles couched in magical terms. A prime example of this is the notion of parallel universes.

A parallel universe is one that exists alongside our own: same people, same places, and same events, but with minor variations. For example, you might exist in two places at once: here, and in an alternate reality where you are slightly shorter and have a different occupation. Or, the alternate reality might enable you to hop between one location (here) and another (the alternate reality). Rather than two of you existing simultaneously, there would be only one you, but you could live on Earth and pop over to your fantasy world at any time.

Getting There

So how does a person pop over to a fantasy world? A very popular anime called *El Hazard* gives us a prime example of how this happens. In this series, three Earth students and an Earth teacher go to a beautiful fantasy world called El Hazard. In this fantasy world, the allied human-ish nations are at war with the insect nation of Bugrom. One of the Earth students, Makoto, first finds the other world by going to some ruins beneath his high school. In these ruins there are light beams, and a mysterious voice tells Makoto to move toward a capsule. As Makoto obeys, he steps beneath what looks like the image of an eye, and suddenly, the light beams encase him. The capsule rises into the air, and then a crying woman totters to Makoto, hugs him, says his name. She says that she has waited ten thousand years for this moment, that she has thought of nothing but Makoto during all those years. She is sending him to El Hazard, she says. Of course, he hasn't a clue where or what El Hazard is, but rather than tell him, the woman generates a beam of white light that transports not only Makoto, but also his classmates Jinnai and Nananmi, as well as his teacher, Mr. Fujisawa, to El Hazard. As the four Earth people are going to El Hazard, faces and planets pass by.

They awaken in a huge forest. Strange creatures, such as dolphin-bears and giant bugs, are everywhere. El Hazard also has castles, evil queens, priestesses, shrines, and princesses. In fact, it turns out that Mr. Fujisawa, a sake drunkard on Earth, has superhuman strength on El Hazard. So in the case of *El Hazard*, people move from Earth to a fantasy world and live in an alternate reality. They do this by going through a doorway of sorts, in this case through some ruins and a light beam beneath a high school.

In *Magic Knights Rayearth*, a stranger method of transport occurs. Here, three girls are on a school field trip to Tokyo Tower when a voice calls to them. Instantly, they teleport to a mystic land called Cefiro. As they fall from the sky toward the ground of Cefiro, a magical beast flies out from the clouds to save them. A five- hundred-year-old little boy named Clef shows up and explains that people control everything about their lives on Cefiro. The person with the most powerful control over her own life is Princess Emurald, he says, and when Cefiro is in great danger, she will summon warriors to fight the evil Zagato. As with *El Hazard, Magic Knights Rayearth* features an alternate reality world, magical beasts, priests (or priestesses), evil versus good, and princesses.

The popular series *Fushigi Yuugi* has been around since 1988 in manga form. In 1995, the series hit the television screen in the form of anime. In this series, junior high students Yuuki Miaka and Hongo Yui find a mysterious book, *The Four Gods of the Earth and Sky*, at the library. The book is about a young girl who is transported to a magical, faraway land in ancient China. As Miaka and Yui read the story, they are magically transported to the fantasy world of the book. After some escapades in the fantasy world, Yui disappears and ends up back on Earth in the library, where she continues reading the book. She gradually realizes that Miaka is magically linked to the book and is experiencing all the events that the book describes. Indeed, Yui is magically linked to Miaka, as well. In this alternate reality story, a person in the fantasy world affects a person back on Earth. If Miaka is hurt, for example, Yui finds blood on her own clothes.

The basic idea is that there exist alternate worlds that are a lot like Earth. This implies that there's intelligent life on other planets. The animes also imply that we can exist on these other planets while we're here on Earth, or we can pop from Earth to these fantasy worlds and back again. So how realistic is all this? Is it possible?

The Science of Parallel Universes

In simple terms, what are parallel worlds? Is it possible to travel to parallel worlds, and if so, how is it done?[74]

Scientists now believe that there might be an infinite number of parallel universes containing "space, time, and other forms of exotic matter."[75] And some of these universes might contain versions of us: that is, you might be sitting in your easy chair right now on planet Earth, reading this book, while another "you" is on another Earthlike planet, flying a helicopter. The other "you" is just like the you on Earth, only slightly different. Perhaps the other "you" has a bigger nose, curly hair, and a sharp temper. Of if the "you" reading this book has a big nose, curly hair, and a sharp temper, then the other "you" might have a tiny nose, straight hair, and a calm demeanor.

According to *Scientific American*, the "simplest and most popular cosmological model today predicts that you have a twin in a galaxy about 10 to the 10^{28}meters from here."[76] Scientists use elementary probability to calculate this estimate; basically, they figure that outer space is infinite and filled with matter in a near-uniform way. Inhabited planets, where extraterrestrials walk, talk, work, and play, are everywhere, and our twins, people who are just like us, with the same appearances, the same memories, and even the same names, are scattered throughout the galaxies.[77]

Today's astronomers can see objects that are approximately 13.7 billion lightyears from Earth, an amount of space known as the Hubble Volume. This volume is approximately the size of our entire universe. Each infinite parallel universe has its own Hubble Volume. About 10 to the 10^{92} meters away is a sphere that has a radius of 100 light years. This sphere is identical to the sphere that is centered here in our universe. Everything that someone sees in that other universe should be the same as everything we see here. Approximately 10 to the 10^{118} meters away is an entire Hubble Volume that is identical to the one you're in right now. Further, each universe is part of a gigantic multiverse.

The idea of the multiverse is "grounded in well-tested theories such as relativity and quantum mechanics,"[78] and the question is not whether the multiverse exists, but rather, how many levels exist within the multiverse.

Every parallel universe that contains a near-identical you is thought to be a Level 1 multiverse. Oddly enough, the Level 1 multiverse is used routinely by cosmologists.

If we live in a Level 1 multiverse, then it's possible that an infinite number of Level 1 multiverses exist. Each would differ from the others, and collectively, all would be known as a Level 2 multiverse. A theory called chaotic eternal inflation is behind the idea of the Level 2 multiverse.

In 1998, supernova observations reinforced the idea that the universe is expanding. Since then, detailed observations of cosmic background radiation have further confirmed it. Scientists believe that space is stretching—hence the use of the word *inflation* in the theory of "chaotic eternal inflation." The accelerating cosmic expansion may be due to the amount of dark energy per cubic centimeter. If scientists knew where dark energy comes from and why it exists in such massive proportions, humans might unlock the secrets behind cosmic expansion. It's been postulated that events in empty space trigger the existence of dark energy. Quantum theory tells us that empty space really isn't "empty"; rather, it consists of virtual particles that "wink in and out of existence so rapidly we can never pin them down directly, but can only observe their effects."[79]

As for *chaotic eternal,* this refers to what happens when space stops stretching in some spots and forms bubbles, until an infinite number of bubbles exist. These bubbles are all different due to the breaking of symmetry. According to one version of this theory, space in our universe once had nine dimensions, but long ago, three of these dimensions evolved during cosmic inflation and became the three dimensions we observe today. This three-dimensional view, or surface, is called a membrane, or brane. The other six dimensions are unobservable, but they do exist. The symmetry that originally existed among the nine dimensions broke when the three observable dimensions split from the other six. Further, the fluctuations that caused chaotic inflation in our universe would cause symmetry breaks in a variety of ways in other universes. The breaks might occur with four observable dimensions, for example.

In simple terms, a dimension is a number that describes a position or motion. To identify the location of an object in space, you use three numbers: latitude, longitude, and altitude. For movement, you can use three directions: forward-backward, up-down, and left-right. Space also has three dimensions, with time being the fourth dimension that creates what we commonly call space-time.

Physicists today suggest that all of the extra dimensions, the ones we can't see, are extremely tiny. Possibly the extra dimensions are rolled up into tiny objects that are even smaller than atoms. These hidden dimensions may be the keys to the origin of the universe, the existence of dark matter, and the doors to parallel universes.

In his 2005 book *Parallel Worlds*, Michio Kaku writes that scientists today are using high-speed supercomputers, gravity wave detectors, space satellites, lasers, interferometers, and other high-tech instruments to deliver the "most compelling description yet" of the creation of the universe. Indeed, writes Kaku, scientists are now speculating that the biblical Genesis "occurs repeatedly in a timeless ocean of Nirvana" and that "our universe may be compared to a bubble floating in a much larger 'ocean,' with new bubbles forming all the time. According to this theory, universes, like bubbles forming in boiling water, are in continual creation, floating in a much larger arena, the Nirvana of eleven-dimensional hyperspace. A growing number of physicists suggest that our universe did indeed spring forth from a fiery cataclysm, the big bang, but that it also coexists in an eternal ocean of other universes."[80]

In addition to theories that predict multiverses far away from us are theories that predict multiverses right in front of our noses. These multiverses are of the type featured in *His Dark Materials*, the popular series of fantasy novels written by Philip Pullman. Open a window into another universe that's sitting right in front of you, and *pop*, you're there.

This type of multiverse theory is known as the "many worlds" interpretation of quantum mechanics; you can think of this theory as the "Level 3 quantum many worlds multiverse." Basically, this theory states that random quantum fluctuations occur that cause our universe to branch into infinite multiple copies of itself. For every question you answer, another you could have answered it in another way. For every hair on your chin, another you might have the same hair on another chin, only a micrometer away.

An entire field of literature has grown out of the idea of quantum many worlds. Parallel universe fiction usually doesn't focus on the events creating the new universes, but rather on what happens after the new universes exist. For example, popular stories center on what the world would have been like if the South had won the Civil War or if the American Revolution had failed and the United States was still a British colony. While not all parallel world stories deal with wars, the concept is popular with military science fiction writers because wars usually feature key moments in which a decision going one way or another has a profound effect on the future. In Ward Moore's parallel world novel *Bring the Jubilee,* the main character travels back in time to change history by making sure the South doesn't win the Civil War. In Ray Bradbury's classic story "A Sound of Thunder," a man who time-travels back to the age of the dinosaurs changes modern history by accidentally stepping on a butterfly millions of years in the past.

Even if we consider the major events in history as moments when the universe branches into two new realities, the number is staggering. How many major events have occurred in human history? Thousands, tens of thousands, hundreds of thousands, millions? Plus, every time a new reality is created, events in its future will also result in parallel worlds. And this branching effect has been going on since the beginning of history. So the branches number in the billions of billions.[81]

As Ray Bradbury suggested in "The Sound of Thunder," even the smallest change in the Jurassic age could have changed all of history that came afterward. The first volcanic eruption on the newly formed Earth might have affected the air we breathe today. Every event that has ever happened must be analyzed when determining how many parallel worlds might exist, and what they're like. The number of parallel universes that exist in direct relationship to our own world is a function of the number of events that have taken place since the creation of Earth.[82]

The many worlds interpretation was first proposed by Hugh Everett III when he was a Princeton graduate student in 1957. According to Everett's theory, whenever multiple possibilities exist in quantum events, the world splits into many worlds, one for each possibility. These worlds are all real and exist simultaneously with the first, while remaining unobservable by any of the others.

Everett's theory is not well liked by many physicists who prefer the Copenhagen Interpretation of Quantum Mechanics, developed by Niels Bohr and Werner Heisenberg in the late 1920s in Copenhagen. The Copenhagen Interpretation says that in quantum mechanics, measurement outcomes are basically indeterministic. Albert Einstein was a strong opponent of the Copenhagen Interpretation, expressing his doubts in the famous line, "God does not play dice."[83]

While the Copenhagen Interpretation is fascinating, we'll stick with the even more interesting many worlds theory. Working with that concept, we find that the number of alternate universes for Earth, while incredibly large, is actually finite, since Earth has not existed forever. If we had a gigantic computer and a lot of spare time for calculating, we could come up with the number of all possible quantum events that have taken place since Earth was formed. We could thus calculate every possible parallel universe created by those events. From there, we could track down every possible quantum event that took place in all these branch universes. Continuing outward, following every possible branch, counting quantum events at the speed of light, we could record billions upon billions of probability worlds that are linked to the first quantum action on Earth. The number would be mind-boggling. Still, the sum of an immense but finite group of immense finite numbers is a finite number. So, though the voyage would be staggering, since the number of universes created by Earth over its billions of years of history is finite, we could travel from the first created parallel universe to the last. Science fiction stories that discuss the details of traveling across millions upon millions of parallel universes include work by Poul Anderson, Andre Norton, H. Beam Piper, and Keith Laumer.

But is that immensely huge number the total of all parallel universes that exist? We've dealt with the many worlds theory as it relates only to Earth. However, the Earth is just one planet, part of one solar system, part of one galaxy, part of one galaxy cluster, part of our universe. Since the entire universe contains atoms whose particles are subject to the laws of quantum mechanics, every atom in the universe is subject to the many worlds theory. While the life cycle of planets, stars, and even galaxies is finite, our current theory about the universe states that it began with a big bang billions of years ago and has been expanding ever since, creating new stars, new solar systems, and new galaxies as it does. As we understand it, the universe is infinite in size. Thus, we have an infinite number of atomic particles whose movement creates parallel universes throughout the entire universe. In other words, since there are an infinite number of atomic particles, there are an infinite number of parallel universes.

The many worlds interpretation also ranges back to the Schrödinger equation. Austrian physicist Erwin Schrödinger (1887–1961) was a pioneer of quantum physics. He devised a famous, yet imaginary, experiment involving a cat. Schrödinger noted that when an atom decays, there might be a 1 in 10 chance that it will decay in thirty minutes, a 9 in 10 chance that it will decay within one day, and so forth. Further, if you're observing the atom at a particular moment, it's either decaying or it isn't decaying; at that moment, there is a 50-50 chance that the atom is decaying. The atom is in a "confused" state, not knowing whether to decay or not decay within that particular moment. Now what if you're not watching the atom?

Schrödinger suggested that, in an imaginary experiment, we might put a "confused" radioactive atom in a locked box with a living cat. The atom alone could not hurt the cat, but if the decay of the atom triggered some sort of killing device, then, should the atom decay, the poor cat would be killed. When the atom is in the 50-50 state, is the cat dead or alive?

The Copenhagen Interpretation mandates that nothing is real unless you look at it. So if you open the box and look at the cat, you'll know whether it's dead or alive. However, if nobody opens the door and looks at the cat, then there's no way to know whether the cat is dead or alive during the moment when the atom is in its 50-50 "confused" state. You could say that the cat is dead and alive at the same time.

In terms of the many worlds interpretation, what Schrödinger's cat theory tells us is that all the parallel universes are real, even though we can't see them. The cat is both dead and alive at the same time: in one world, the cat is alive, and in another world, the cat is dead. If you exist in this world, open the box, and see a live cat, then another you in another world is opening the box and seeing a dead cat.

And each time anything in the quantum realm has a choice—to decay or not to decay, for example—the universe splits in this way. All of these parallel universes exist simultaneously.

The multiverse theory suggests that different laws of nature might exist on infinite worlds. It also suggests that life might exist—in fact, probably does exist—on many other worlds. As *National Geographic* points out in its lead article for December 2004, "Astronomers are more certain than ever that other planets like our own exist in the universe. Now they just have to find them."[84] And as Michio Kaku writes in January 2005, "Physicists and astronomers around the world are now speculating about what these parallel worlds may look like, what laws they might obey, how they are born, and how they may eventually die. . . . Perhaps they look just like our universe, separated by a single quantum event that made these universes diverge from ours. . . . The engine driving these new theories is the massive flood of data that is pouring in from our space satellites as they photograph remnants of creation itself."[85]

8. The Future of Virtual Reality

The World of *dot hack sign*

You wake up on the side of a mountain. The clothes you are wearing are unfamiliar: robes, garments that seem wrong, but you can't remember what would be right. You're carrying what seems to be a heavy sword. Touching it, you realize that you know how to wield it, a skill that somehow does not seem natural. Your mind is filled with many questions, but you have no answers.

Concentrating, you remember a name. Tsukasa. That's you, and you're a boy. These feeling are all very strange. There's more to this than you can understand. Your mind seems to be working fine. You comprehend things, but you seem to be lacking any memories of where you are and why you are there.

Soon, you encounter a young woman warrior armed with a huge sword. Her name is Mimiru and she seems friendly. Still, you know nothing about her, so you use your powers to disappear. You're not sure exactly how you do that, but somehow you can move from one area of this place, this unknown world, to another by the mere motion of your hands. After traveling around a bit, from forest to mountains to a city with canals, you end up back on the mountain where you started. A knight dressed in scarlet tells you that you're breaking the rules of the world and attacks you. But he's defeated by a guardian that appears out of nowhere. It's all quite odd and it makes no sense. You hope life will get less confusing soon.

Needless to say, things don't get better for Tsukasa, though he does find a number of friends who want to help. More than most anime adventures shown over the past few years in Japan, *.hack//SIGN*, known to most fans as *dot hack sign,* has a very complex plot line. *Dot hack sign* ran on TV in Japan in 2002–2003. It was written by Kazunori Ito and Omode Akemi, and it was directed by Koichi Mashimo. Along with the TV series, there

were four *dot hack sign* video games created for Playstation 2 that tied in closely to the plot. And needless to say, there was a manga, though it was started after the show was already on the air.

The science behind this story is called virtual reality, or VR. According to online dictionaries, VR is a computer simulation that uses 3-D graphics and sometimes physical devices such as goggles, earphones, and gloves to allow the user to interact with the simulation.[86]

In other words, virtual reality creates high-tech illusions. It's a computer-generated, three-dimensional environment that engulfs the senses of sight, sound, and touch. Once the environment is entered, it "becomes" reality to the user. Within this virtual world, users travel and interact with objects that are wholly the products of a computer or avatars of other participants in the same environment. The limits of this virtual environment depend almost entirely on the sophistication and capabilities of the computer and the software that drives the system.

Because virtual reality users remain stationary, they normally use a joystick or trackball to move through the virtual environment. Users also may wear a special glove or use other devices to manipulate objects within the virtual world.

The setting for *dot hack sign* is called "The World," and that's all the name it needs. That's because for those who inhabit it, that's exactly what it is, an entire world for online gamers to engage in a massive multiplayer online role-playing game (MMORPG). The world is a swords-and-sorcery realm, very similar to the setting for

THE SCIENCE OF ANIME

the Final Fantasy video games, where people can design their own characters and give them armor and weapons, as well as special skills and characteristics. It's a place where players' avatars wander around a gigantic landscape consisting of deserts, mountains, cities, castles, and forests, gathering hit points and experience points to raise their skills and powers. The World is inhabited by monsters and talking animals, and it's filled with treasure chests, rare gems, and extra-powerful weapons. Like most MMORPG, players can gather together into teams to go on quests, using their different powers to aid the group's survival. This particular World is patrolled by a bunch of volunteers called the Crimson Knights, who log into the game as a clan of peacekeepers to ensure that everything runs smoothly online. As with all MMORPG, you can log in for a few hours after school or work, have some exciting adventures with your character, and then log out for the evening. Except if you're Tsukasa. Because for some unknown reason, he can't remember looking down at his keyboard. And he can't seem to log out of the game.

The plot of *dot hack sign* is deceptively simple. A player is caught in the game and can't get out. A group of other players, all of whom understand that the game is not real, can't understand why Tsukasa can't sign off and want to help him. To do so, they must explore areas of the game they've never before visited, areas that perhaps were not meant to be seen. As the story develops, we learn that some of the players have reasons for playing the game that have little to do with entertainment. Most of the characters lead drab, everyday lives in the real world, and playing in the game enables them to be the type of character they've always wanted to be. A few lead a cruel existence in the real world, and the game offers them excitement instead of harsh reality. None of the players can figure out how Tsukasa can remain in the game all the time. Everyone has to take a break from the cyber-reality of the game to eat, sleep, and, in most cases, go to work or school. There's only so much time even a hard-core game player can spend in the World. Except, it seems, for Tsukasa.

The secondary lead in the game is a young woman named Subaru. Subaru is the leader of the Crimson Knights. She is a gentle character and rarely fights—thus, her level is very low. She is often the voice of reason and peace—a character who wants all to be happy—yet "right." She spends a lot of time in The World—most likely to escape her unhappy life in the real world.

Subaru is not a typical MMORPG player. She seems unconcerned about fighting monsters or finding treasures. Nor is she interested in raising her battle level to make herself more powerful. Instead, Subaru appears to be simply living in the alternate world and taking things that happen there seriously.

The relationship that develops between Tsukasa and Subaru turns out to be the most important plot element of *dot hack sign*. The World is a place where all players start out equal. There are no special benefits for players who in real life have extraordinary athletic skills or immense amounts of money. Young and old, everyone is the same age in The World. Nor does it matter what country a player comes from or what his or her reason for playing the game is. Everyone is equal in cyberspace, which makes it a true vision of utopia—complete with dragons, ogres, swords, and spells.

The true measure of *dot hack sign* is not the adventures that the various characters go on in their attempt to solve the mystery of Tsukasa. Instead, the depth and meaning of the series is revealed as the viewer learns the true nature of the people behind the avatars. The basic truth of the anime is that it's all about the players and not about the game. The closing scene of the series, when Tsukasa and Subaru meet in the real world, is one of the most compelling and poignant moments in any science fiction anime produced in the past ten years.

The underlying concept of *dot hack sign* is the possibilities virtual reality holds for now and for the future. In telling Tsukasa's story, the anime shows in vivid terms how game immersion doesn't always have to be self-destructive. For too many years, virtual reality has been seen as an interesting novelty without much real use. That's no longer the case, and developments in the field point to major developments in the use of VR in our daily lives over the next hundred years. *dot hack sign* was a small preview of what amazing transformation virtual reality will bring to our lives. And in the not-too-distant future.

Virtual Surgery

In her article "Whatever Happened to Virtual Reality?" published in *NewsFactor Technology News* on August 30, 2002, Elizabeth Millard raised the important question that many other computer engineers had been afraid to mention for the past decade. Less than ten years ago, it seemed as though virtual reality was set to become the next major breakthrough in modern electronics. At the time, most VR work seemed to center around game arcades, with VR shooting games getting all the attention. Then, without even a word of farewell, the games disappeared, the articles dried up, and the virtual reality field vanished like snow in the desert.

What happened was that this exciting field hit the brick wall of higher-than-expected costs and lower-than-projected returns. Virtual reality products were expensive, and the amount of funding needed for research and development was vast beyond imagination. The VR world retreated to its birthplace, college campuses, where work could be done using special grants that employed graduate students as the grunts and developed big ideas in small ways.

Virtual reality had ridden in on a wave of hype, telling people that it would produce a total immersive experience that would make gaming a joy, hunting a pleasure, and, would train new recruits in everything from warfare to brain surgery, injury-free and affordable. Companies promised products for the kitchen that would turn time spent there into a science fiction experience. Unfortunately, the reality never even came close to these projections.[87]

According to Rob Enderle, an analyst at Giga Information Group, VR was short-circuited by a problem that no one had anticipated. "People became physically ill," he said, "when using head-mounted displays." The motion sickness was quite common, and most virtual reality projects came to a complete stop. "They are working on the causes of the [motion sickness] and clearly we will solve these problems going forward," added Enderle. "But since this is more medical than technical, it may take a while."[88]

Computers at present are not fast enough to process huge amounts of graphic information in real time. In a virtual environment, frames are displayed at a rate of about seven per second, an extremely slow speed when compared to a television, which generates sixty frames per second. The human eye processes images much faster than a computer. Thus, most users find VR images choppy or slow. These slow graphics produce what is known as simulator sickness. This disorder causes the user to experience disorientation and nausea, somewhat akin to motion sickness. Simulator sickness occurs because the eyes are accustomed to real-world speeds. About 10 percent of all VR users are affected by simulator sickness. In the future, as computers speed up and process graphic information more quickly, this number should drop toward zero.[89]

Another reason that virtual reality seemed to go nowhere after its initial buildup days was the aforementioned lack of funding. Large-scale, tech-intensive projects required cash—and lots of it. Not many companies were willing to risk huge amounts of money in unproven, unorthodox science. The only ones who remained were those few large firms specializing in new applications for heavy industry. According to Enderle, "the most important work being done in VR is in the military and aerospace industries. "There are still companies in 2005 that are trying to make VR a commercial success in areas other than the military," he said. "But these companies are not devoting as many resources as they once did. Sony for example, is working in the field, but not as aggressively as it did in the early days.

"We are likely ten to fifteen years off from what I might call a real virtual reality experience," Enderle said. "The technology is almost there, but getting it into a form we can afford, and live with, will take a while.[90]

Fortunately, Rob Enderle doesn't work in the medical field, because if he did, his opinions would have gotten him fired a long time ago. In fact, VR is reshaping the face of medicine and is touted as one of the greatest medical technological breakthroughs of all time. And, it's not an invention for ten or fifteen years from now. VR operations are saving lives as this book is being written.

In the 1990s various research teams, notably at the University of North Carolina and at the U.S. Department of Defense, came up with the idea that surgeons of the future wearing virtual reality headsets could rehearse real or robotic procedures using advanced computer-generated images. At the same time, the growing field of virtual reality technology pushed the idea of medical simulation among the major VR companies in the United States. Unfortunately, most of those programs went nowhere.

However, recent conferences such as "Medicine Meets Virtual Reality 2003," held in the United States, suggest that some goals have been reached. Established products are becoming available at affordable prices for most surgical teaching institutions. In addition, many projects are now receiving academic grant support or U.S. or European Union funding.[91]

Virtual reality in medicine is a collection of technologies that allow people to interact efficiently with 3-D computerized databases in real time using their natural senses and skills. Forget special helmets and instrumented clothing such as gloves or suits, as was the case in the late 1980s and early 1990s. Immersive technology, as it is called, is still used today, but only in about 10 percent of virtual reality applications. The key component of virtual reality is that it supports and enhances real time interaction on the part of the user.

The application of this technology to surgical training is easy to understand. Surgical training is expensive, and the pressures from shortened training programs and reduced working hours for trainees require that an increasing amount of practice be done outside the actual operating theater. What must be proven with VR technology is that using it for training serves as well as work with real patients. Recent evidence supports this. Not only has the virtual reality community produced experimentally validated systems for the training and assessment of surgical skills, it has done so using established techniques that are now becoming recognized as international standards—such as the International Organization for Standardization's ISO 13407, "Human-centred design processes for interactive systems."[92]

Obviously, there's a big difference for surgical trainees between training with artificial or inanimate tissues (such as raw chicken) and supervised procedures on patients in the operating theater, with all the attendant pressures such as time restraints and clinical governance. A commercially available simulator for venepuncture has force feedback to simulate the feel of the cannula entering the skin and vein. This is suitable for training nurses, medical students, phlebotomists, and paramedics. More complex simulators for therapeutic gastroscopy, endoscopic retrograde cholangiopancreatography, and colonoscopic procedures are available for trainees in gastroenterology. A radiological simulator provides training in cardiac catheterization and angiography, with real-time modeling of physiological parameters and blood flow. These virtual reality simulators offer repeatable, monitored computerized training, often without any need for supervision.[93]

Also, some interactive virtual reality simulators that have been developed for procedures such as lumbar puncture and brain ventricular tap are freely available for use over the Internet.

Not only is VR becoming increasingly important in the training of doctors and nurses, it has also become an important tool in the training and rehabilitation of stroke patients. As part of a small study in Dallas, Texas, stroke victims played virtual reality games in which they imagined they were diving with sharks or snowboarding down a narrow slope; as a result, their ability to walk eventually improved, researchers reported. Doctors called the findings promising, especially since the patients had all had strokes more than a year earlier, a time frame in which further recovery is unlikely.

"People love to play games," said study coauthor Dr. Mark Hallett. The virtual reality therapy helped the patients use their weakened legs and ultimately walk better. Hallett is chief of the human motor-control section with the National Institute of Neurological Disorders and Stroke.[94] The sample size of the study was small—ten people—and the volunteers were comparatively young, with an average age of fifty-seven. Researchers believe video games may be a good way to keep patients engaged in therapy. About 700,000 people each year experience a new or recurrent stroke, which often impairs one side of the body and walking ability. The patients in the study, which appeared in the May 13, 2005 issue of the magazine *Stroke,* all had weakness on one side of their body. Researchers randomly assigned them to a control group or a virtual reality group. The control group got no intervention, while the virtual reality group used the video training for an hour a day, five days a week, for more than a month.

"This was a group of people that you would not expect to improve, and that's what made it interesting that they did," said

Dr. Robert Felberg, director of the stroke program at Ochsner Clinic Foundation in New Orleans. In the three games used in the study, the patient's body is superimposed onto the scene. Range of motion, balance, mobility, stepping, and walking skills are all targeted. One game simulates going up and down stairs; another lets the patient go deep-sea diving with sharks; and the third re-creates snowboarding by simulating gliding down a narrow slope, jumping, and avoiding obstacles.

The five patients who played the games improved in walking, standing, and climbing steps, researchers said. Also, brain imaging done before and after the experiment indicated a reorganization of brain function after the therapy, said lead author Sung H. You, an assistant professor of physical therapy at Hampton University in Hampton, Virginia.[95]

Virtual reality will play a major role in such important future developments in medicine as microsurgery and nanosurgery. Just as virtual reality was first developed to control macro-scale robots for use in hazardous environments, future microrobots and even nanobots, such as the DNA "screwdriver," designed for use within the human body, will need supervision by skilled operators equipped with advanced virtual reality equipment. A German company has already produced a "micro-submarine" powered by an induction motor. At 4 millimeters long and 650 μm (micrometers, defined as one millionth of a meter) in diameter, the submarine is small enough to pass through the tip of a hypodermic needle. This micro-sub has the potential to perform in numerous diagnostic or therapeutic applications. Miniature cameras that can be swallowed and transmit images of the gastrointestinal tract to a viewing station are being used to survey the digestive system for a variety of diseases.[96]

European and U.S. developments in micro-lasers and micro-manipulators, such as the da Vinci Surgical System, are now being used for master-slave robotic procedures such as minimally invasive coronary artery bypass grafting and laparoscopic surgery. These techniques are proof of the importance of virtual reality technology. Moreover, their use suggests that a revolution in medical instruments and in the training of surgeons to use them is closer to becoming reality than most people realize.

The greatest problem facing VR surgical advances isn't the science, but the medical community itself, which is notorious for not accepting new technology, no matter how great the benefit it offers. Virtual reality and robots are still viewed by most surgeons as gimmicks or potentially dangerous. More multidisciplinary teams will be required to develop the use of these new technologies in surgery. Evidence of the benefits is likely to take at least another five to ten years to become accepted into the mainstream.

Virtual Law Enforcement

Another area in which VR offers great rewards for a relatively small investment is in the field of law enforcement. However, most police agencies seem unaware of the VR simulations available and of the benefits of using them to train new officers. In a long, detailed article titled "Virtual Reality: The Future of Law Enforcement Training," Jeffrey S. Hormann, an FBI agent in charge of the U.S. Army Criminal Investigation Command, Fort Belvoir, Virginia, outlines the many benefits that VR offers today's police.

According to Agent Hormann, in today's competitive business environment, major corporations are constantly working to accomplish tasks faster, better, and less expensively. This is particularly true in training, and virtual reality simulation is rapidly emerging as a potential high-tech method of providing realistic, safe, and cost-effective training. For example, a firefighter can battle the flames of a virtual burning building. A police officer can struggle with virtual "shoot/don't shoot" dilemmas. Acting in a virtual environment, trainees can make decisions and act upon them without risk to themselves or others. At the same time, instructors can critique students' actions, enabling them to learn from their mistakes. This capability gives virtual reality a tremendous advantage over most conventional training methods.

The Department of Defense (DOD) leads public and private industry in developing virtual reality training. Since the early 1980s, the DOD has actively researched, developed, and used virtual reality simulations to train members of the armed forces to fight effectively in combat. The DOD's current approach to virtual reality training emphasizes team tactics. Groups of military personnel from around the world engage in combat safely on a virtual battlefield. Combatants never come together physically; rather, simulators located at various sites throughout the world transmit data to a central location, where the virtual battle is controlled. Because it costs less to move information than people, this form of training has proven quite cost-effective.[97]

An additional benefit to this sort of training is that battles can be fought under a variety of conditions. Virtual battlefields can be used to re-create real-world locations with numerous dangerous characteristics. To explore unusual battle scenarios, participants can modify enemy capabilities, the terrain, the weather, and enemy weapon systems.

Virtual reality can even re-create actual battles. Based on information from participants, the Institute for Defense Analyses re-created the Second Armored Cavalry Regiment offensive conducted in Iraq during Operation Desert Storm. The success of the virtual re-creation was obvious when soldiers who had participated in that battle reported the extreme accuracy of the re-creation and the feeling of reliving the battle.

Virtual reality holds great potential for accurate review and analysis of real-world situations that would be difficult to accomplish by any other method. Several important studies have shown that military units perform better following virtual reality training. Even though virtual environments are only simulations, VR immersion overwhelms most users, engrossing them in the action. This realism plays a major role in a program's success. In the future, the DOD plans to train infantry personnel individually with virtual reality fighting-skill simulators.

The success of virtual reality as a training and planning tool for the military makes it obvious that there are many potential applications for this technology in other fields. Many military uses can easily be translated into law enforcement techniques, for example, including training in firearms, stealth tactics, and assault skills.

Unfortunately, few VR manufacturers have developed virtual reality programs for law enforcement. According to a recently published resource guide, more than 100 companies are currently selling virtual reality hardware or software. Not one of these firms mentions law enforcement in their advertising or promotions. Furthermore, a search on the Internet found numerous articles on virtual reality technology, but only a very few that addressed law-enforcement applications. Yet, virtual reality obviously offers law enforcement important benefits in a number of areas, including pursuit driving, firearms training, high-risk incident management, incident re-creation, and crime-scene processing.[98]

Too often, young police officers don't get a chance to learn from their mistakes. Surviving the streets requires training that prepares them for deadly situations they might suddenly and unexpectedly encounter on patrol. Since many training programs emphasize repetition to teach the right response, they often don't cover unexpected scenarios. The more realistic the training, the better the lesson.

"Virtual reality can provide the type of training that today's law-enforcement officers need. By completely immersing the senses in a computer-generated environment, the artificial world becomes reality to users and greatly enhances their training experiences,"[99] according to FBI Agent Hormann.

Pursuit driving is one area in which a virtual reality has become a reality for the police. Law-enforcement personnel identified a need and provided input to a major VR manufacturer that developed a driving simulator equipped with realistic controls. The simulator provides users with realistic steering-wheel feedback, road feel, and other vehicle motions. The screen has a standard 225-degree field of view, with 360-degree coverage optional.

Simulations can involve one or more drivers, and environments can alternate between city streets, rural roads, and oval tracks. The vehicle itself can change from a police car to a truck, ambulance, or other car. Virtual reality driving simulators provide police departments invaluable training at a fraction of the long-term cost of using actual vehicles. In fact, the simulator is being used by a number of police departments around the country.

During the past several years, the Los Angeles County Sheriff's Office Emergency Vehicle Operations Center (EVOC) has used a four-station version of the driving simulator to train its officers. The simulators help the officers develop judgment and decision-making skills, while providing an environment free from risk of injury or damage to vehicles.[100]

Another law-enforcement area where VR could be used with great success is in shoot/don't shoot training simulations. A virtual reality system would allow officers to enter a three-dimensional environment alone or as a member of a team and confront computer-generated criminals or even other virtual reality users. Evaluators could observe the training from any perspective. Equally useful, training scenarios could involve real floor plans of buildings, including important locations like city hall or local city streets. Other factors, such as weather, number of criminals and police, and types of weapons could be changed as needed.

VR could also be used by SWAT team members before embarking on high-risk tactical assaults. The floor plans and other known facts about a location could be fed into a computer to create a virtual environment for team members to analyze prior to action.

Though virtual reality may appear to be the ideal law-enforcement tool, as with any new technology, there are some drawbacks. Currently, areas of concern range from cumbersome equipment to negative physical and psychological effects experienced by some users. Fortunately, however, the field is evolving and improving constantly. As virtual reality gains widespread use, most major problems with the system will be solved.

Design by VR

We're at an automobile factory in Japan. A large 3-D computer-generated model of a new sedan floats in space in front of a manager's eyes. She presses a button on the stylus she holds in one hand and starts drawing directly onto the surface of the car. When she traces the lines around the wheel wells, she feels resistance against the stylus corresponding to the curves of the steel. It feels like she's pulling a magic marker against the body of a real car.

Meanwhile, thousands of miles away, in Los Angeles, a car designer sees the same lines appearing on the exact same virtual vehicle. He writes a note to himself that he needs to check to see if the fender is too close to the tire. These events aren't happening in the future, but right now. It's virtual reality being used to design automobiles. And it's based on the work of Berkeley mechanical engineering professor Sara McMains.[101]

According to the professor, VR makes perfect sense when using an international team to work on a project: "Instead of having to bring everyone who has a stake in a design together in one physical location, they can be anywhere and still talk about the particulars and provide valuable feedback during the design process."[102]

McMains, along with graduate students Youngung Shon and Irena Nadjakova and professor Carlo Séquin, are testing this new VR system, which enables collaborators to work at great distances from each other. The name of the system is CHaMUE, which stands for Collaborative Haptic Mark-Up Environment. Users put on stereo glasses that provide a three-dimensional view of a computer-generated model displayed on a drafting table–like display screen. The glasses track the wearer's head so he or she can view the model's different angles simply by looking "around" the image. The user can manipulate a special stylus, called a Phantom, hanging from a force-feedback network. The Phantom and the software that makes it work convert digital information about a virtual reality model into force feedback so that it duplicates the sensation of actually touching the real thing. In this situation, the touching consisted of drawing changes on the car model. CHaMUE lets users at workstations scattered throughout the world communicate and interact with each other, as well as with the car model, through the Internet.[103]

The CHaMUE system was designed to work in many different areas. However, Professor McMains has found that the automobile industry has been her biggest client. Many car companies have been relying on overseas companies to design and manufacture many of the parts for their new vehicles; because the companies involved are often separated by thousands of miles, it can be difficult to share information during the design and manufacturing process. Using CHaMUE puts an end to that problem.

Working together over long distances using virtual reality is not a new idea. But usually the models have been either simple, two-dimensional designs or extremely complicated CAD designs[104] that most non-engineers as well as many product managers find difficult to understand. Professor McMains hopes that using CHaMUE will make such work much easier. She also hopes that one day CHaMUE will be used in all sorts of human-computer interactions. "Our hope is that this system would be intuitive and fun so people would be more likely to use it," she declares.[105] It's another step closer to the virtual reality of tomorrow's world.

9. Plausible but Illogical

There's one question guaranteed to start an argument at any comic book or anime convention held in the United States. Ask a crowd of ten to fifteen fans, ranging in age from ten to thirty years old, what's better? Manga or comic books? Anime or animated cartoon shows on American TV? Then take a few steps back and watch the sparks fly. Fans of American comics are fighting a losing battle, because a vast majority of comic books in the United States are aimed at the twelve to twenty-five-year-old-male demographic and are dominated by superheroes and supervillains. These stories are usually high-impact adventures filled with a lot of fights and super science, but are not very deep, emotional, or scientific. They're great fun, but except for a very few graphic novels written and drawn by the very top talent in the business, they are totally forgettable. The cartoons derived from the comics are no better or worse than the stories they bring to life. Two-dimensional comic book characters do not turn into three-dimensional cartoon heroes. It just doesn't happen that way.

Manga's better, simply put, because the stories aren't just about superheroes and supervillains. Many of the stories are told in shades of gray, where the main characters are a curious mix of good and evil in one. While there are always absolutely evil characters floating about in the pages of manga, there are an equal number of misunderstood villains who just want to do the right thing. Anime stories range from cute and silly to adventurous and exciting, to meaningful and philosophical and very, very deep. It's hard to find any cartoons in America that can be labeled as difficult to understand, obtuse, or puzzling. It's often hard to find animes in Japan that are not. It's the nature of the medium, a reflection of the culture.

Science is treated as an important part of anime adventures. In cartoons and comic books produced in the United States, rules of science are routinely ignored, bent, or broken in the quest to tell a good story. That's not the case in Japan, where science serves as an important building block for such anime epics as *Mobile Suit Gundam* and *Neon Genesis Evangelion*. Science hides in the corner every time a new Spiderman or Batman movie is released in the United States.

We're not surprising anyone reading this book with these thoughts. Most American comic book writers and artists would be the first to admit they know very little about science and technology. And they don't feel it's their job to weave modern science into their stories. On the other hand, Japanese writers work hard to include the latest scientific breakthroughs in their stories and strive for the most accurate popular science in their epics. They search for the latest discoveries in space travel, biology, and

genetics to make their stories not only entertaining but scientifi-
cally accurate.

But despite the accurate science and the much-more-adult feel
to the stories, anime is still regarded only as a species of somewhat
more intelligent cartoons by most of its American audience. Only
a few films, such as *Spirited Away* or *Ghost in the Shell,* are treated
like films aimed at adults, and even those are rarely huge hits in
the United States. Despite all the publicity and loud claims that
manga and anime are for adults, in North America, the twin art
forms are still regarded as kids' stuff. Why?

No one knows the answer beyond a shadow of a doubt, but we
can make an intelligent guess. In anime, there's a certain lack of
sophistication. Anime, for all of its scientific accuracy, adult conversation, and violent action, lacks true believability. Furthermore,
anime brings to the table certain innate prejudices that raise an
uncomfortable feeling within the American watcher. Just as
showing a film featuring the hero eating a ham and cheese sand-
wich while drinking a glass of milk would not go over well in
Israel, certain Japanese anime core beliefs do not play well to
American audiences. Until anime corrects these assumptions, the
field will never be a hit on American TV or movie screens like it
is in Japan.

Take government, for example. In the United States, we live in
a democracy where we elect the leaders of our government in free
and open elections. There are three independent branches of
government—the president, the legislature, and the courts, which

maintain a system of checks and balances so that the people are fairly and honestly represented. For all the complaints and disagreements Americans have about and with their government, most of them would admit it works fairly well.

Try to find a democracy in science fiction anime. It's not easy. Most countries in the stories are ruled by aristocrats or the military or a combination of both. There are no representatives of the common people, and the government does just as it wants. In a number of shows, big business runs the country. Or secret corporations have puppet governors rule in their place. Think about it. Who's in charge in *Akira,* in *Neon Genesis Evangelion,* in *Ghost in the Shell,* or in *Mobile Suit Gundam*?

If the rulers aren't dictators or power merchants, then they're aristocracy. Consider the fact that Japan was ruled by an emperor for hundreds of years, until after World War II. Then, with that thought in mind, take a closer look at *Nausicaa of the Valley of the Wind, Metropolis,* and *Escaflowne.* Along with the influence of Japan's royal family, blame *Star Wars* for the princess effect. Since *Star Wars* first appeared on movie screens back in the late 1970s, princesses and imperial senates and emperors and knights have been around in ever-increasing numbers. *Star Wars* might have brought back space opera and romance to the movie screens, but along with it, the series brought along medieval-style governments and tyranny.

Another area where anime stumbles might be called "consequences." While shows explore the latest scientific advances and futuristic ideas with amazing accuracy, they sometimes ignore some of the more important by-products of the technology involved. That's acceptable for a cartoon, but for an anime series that strives to be much more accurate and believable than a mere cartoon show, cause and effect can't be ignored.

Consider *Ghost in the Shell: Stand Alone Complex.* One of the most fascinating subjects covered in depth in the show is the idea that in twenty-five years, or sooner, we'll be able to download our minds to machines or cyborgs. In fact, the main character of the show is a cyborg, a human mind that's been downloaded into a cybernetic cyborg body. It's a terrific idea, well presented and well used in the series. But there's much more to it than is ever mentioned in the show. In fact, there's a whole new branch of the law needed. Soon. To wit: if a human can download his or her mind to a computer, that mind, those thoughts, become part of the computer's memory bank. Then, even if the person is killed, another download can be performed using the uploaded material from before. In a sense, that person—if they don't mind losing a few recent memories—is immortal. It's an idea that's been common to science fiction since it was first introduced in the novel *The World of Null-A* by A. E. van Vogt, published sixty years ago.

Now, take that idea another step forward. A person downloads his or her mind to a computer, then uploads that mind into a cyborg body. A copy of the subject's mind is still in the computer. There's no reason to wipe it out when downloading the data into the cyborg mind. If that's the case, why not download that personality into a second cyborg body at the same time? Or a third? Or ten different bodies? Why not create a cyborg army made up of one person?

One of the episodes of *Stand Alone Complex* deals with a South American revolutionary who returns to Japan every few years to revive another cyborg body for his mind. That's the way he remains young and fearless for his aging followers. We ask, why bother pretending to be the same man? Why not instead have fifteen or twenty revolutionaries roaming the countryside stirring up trouble, all with the body and mind of the original? It's perfectly logical if you accept the initial concept of downloading your mind onto a computer.

Still another Pandora's box opened by the *Stand Alone Complex* series is that if people can download their minds to a computer, then wouldn't the world become filled with immortals? Once your mind is loaded onto a computer, you can download it again and again, no matter how many times you're killed or die from some disease. It's a scenario discussed in many science fiction novels. If the world goes digital, will there be enough room for everyone to live on the planet—since nobody dies? Again, it's a serious topic that can't be ignored—and yet it is, in *Ghost in the Shell: Stand Alone Complex.*

Let's switch shows and switch subjects. Early on in *Akira,* we're told that Tokyo was destroyed by a mysterious atomic bomb that started World War III. Later on, we learn that there was no bomb, and that the blast was caused by Akira using his incredible mental powers. That's OK, but it forces us to ask, exactly how did the war really start? Who blamed who for launching the nuclear bomb? Or was it just assumed that the bomb was smuggled into Tokyo? Why didn't the general who was in charge of the Akira project tell the government that it wasn't actually a nuclear blast instead of letting his country be attacked? *Akira* only makes sense if you don't ask any questions about it.

Ditto *Neon Genesis Evangelion,* with its explosion in Antarctica that wipes out half the people on Earth. Yet no one seems to wonder about the blast, or why a meteor impact never caused such damage before. When we watch any of the *Mobile Suit Gundam* adventures, we're painfully aware that before the start of the series, five billion people have been killed. *Five billion?* And yet the war rages on? There's a casual attitude to hundreds of millions of people dying that seems to be perfectly acceptable to anime characters that doesn't ring true to life. Japan is the only country ever to feel the impact of nuclear weapons. Tens of thousands of people were killed by atomic bombs. Doesn't it seem strange that anime suggests that the death of billions of people would only result in a truce in the war for a week?

The problem with science fiction anime is that it wants to be accepted as intelligent, well-written movie and television material, but at the same time it wants to play by animation rules. That no longer works. A good show takes topics and explores them completely. A bad show just glides on through. Being plausible isn't enough. A good show needs to be logical as well. Because, without logic, nothing in science makes much sense.

There's no question that anime is part of the digital revolution in entertainment. The only question that remains is whether it will be in the forefront of that revolution or struggling in the pack.

In Closing

Well, it's been a fun trip, but now it's coming to a close. We've enjoyed writing about some of our favorite anime shows and movies and hope you've been entertained and maybe learned something interesting along the way. We still don't understand *Neon Genesis Evangelion,* despite having watched it four times through; we feel sorry for Subaru from *dot hack sign;* and we can't wait to see the entire second season of *Ghost in the Shell.* No question about it, we're not just science writers; we love anime and it was a kick getting a chance to put down some of our thoughts on our favorite shows. We appreciate you buying this book and, if we could, we'd thank you all in person. Since that's not possible, consider this short afterword our way of doing just that. Thanks! We really do appreciate your support!

Have a question or a comment about the book? You can contact us online at www.robertweinberg.net or www.sff.net/people/lgresh. We do try to answer all our email, but please be patient. Sometimes it takes us a while to get to your letters, especially if we're working on another book. And we're usually working on another book.

Thanks again for reading.

Lois H. Gresh
Robert Weinberg
May 15, 2005

Notes

1. See http://news.bbc.co.uk/1/hi/sci/tech/1112411.stm.
2. See http://www.rnw.nl/science/html/robots000807.html.
3. Ibid.
4. See http://www.sciencenews.org/20010630/bob8.asp.
5. Ibid.
6. See http://www.dailycal.org/article.asp?id=7517.
7. "James Bond's Gadgets," *Hot Topics: Science of James Bond,* November 15, 2002, http://www.bbc.co.uk/science/hottopics/jamesbond/ bondgadgets.html.
8. See http://www.oandp.com/news/.
9. Nighswonger, Greg, "New Polymers and Nanotubes Add Muscle to Prosthetic Limbs," *Medical Device & Diagnostic Industry Magazine,* August 1999.
10. This copolymer material is used in blood storage bags.
11. Nighswonger, Greg, ibid.
12. We're going to quote ourselves again. Gresh, Lois H., *TechnoLife 2020: A Day in the World of Tomorrow,* (ECW Press, 2001), 185–195. And also: Gresh and Weinberg, *The Science of James Bond,* (John Wiley & Sons, 2002), *The Science of Supervillains* (Wiley, 2004), and *The Science of Superheroes,* (Wiley, 2002).
13. See the Biomimetic Products, Inc., Web site at http://www.biomimetic.com/faq.html.
14. "Smart Materials," *Scientific American,* May 1996.
15. See http://endo.sandia.gov/9234/smas.html.
16. Zey, Michael G., *The Future Factor: The Five Forces Transforming Our Lives and Shaping Human Destiny,* (McGraw-Hill, 2000), 84. Zey is the executive director of the Expansionary Institute, a consultant to Fortune 500 companies and government agencies.
17. O'Malley, Chris "The Binary Man: Step One," *Popular Science,* March 1999.

18. "Tech 2010," *New York Times Magazine,* June 11, 2000.
19. See http://www.sciam.com/askexpert/chemistry/chemistry6.html.
20. Drexler, as quoted in Gross, *Travels to the Nanoworld: Miniature Machinery in Nature and Technology,* 199. Gross has a doctorate in physical biochemistry.
21. See http://www.sciam.com/askexpert/chemistry/chemistry6.html.
22. "Tech 2010," *New York Times Magazine.*
23. Anderson, "Mega Steps Toward the Nanochip," *Wired* magazine.
24. Gross, *Travels to the Nanoworld: Miniature Machinery in Nature and Technology,* 153. Carbon nanotubes have been the subject of many fascinating articles in scientific magazines and journals during the past few years. Gross provides a brief and excellent introduction to the subject in his book. He writes, "Historically, carbon nanotubes are a byproduct of the phenomenon that became known as the *fullerene fever.* After Wolfgang Kratschmer's group at the Max Planck Institute for Nuclear Physics in Heidelberg had described a recipe suitable for the mass production of these soccer ball–shaped molecules, fullerene chemistry spread epidemically (quite literally, as the increase in publications and citations was successfully modeled using the mathematical descriptions developed for epidemics). One of the first scientists infected was Sumio Iijima, who worked in the research laboratories of NEC in Tsukuba, Japan. While trying to optimize his procedures to produce fullerenes, he slightly changed the technical parameters in his discharge apparatus and was surprised to find that instead of soccer balls he obtained long and thin fibrils. Electron microscopy revealed these fibers to consist of concentrically stacked graphite cylinders, whose ends were capped with fullerene-like hemispheres. Like the fullerenes, these tubes represented a novel modification of carbon. As their diameters typically measured a few nanometers, they became generally known as *carbon nanotubes,* or less formally, as *buckytubes.*"
25. Anderson, "Becoming Your Own Hospital," *Wired* magazine.
26. Swissler, "Microchips to Monitor Meds," *Wired* magazine.
27. See http://www.robothalloffame.org/.
28. We're taking the liberty of quoting from our earlier books, *The Computers of Star Trek* (Basic Books, 1999) and *The Science of Supervillians* (John Wiley & Sons, 2004).
29. Brooks, "Elephants Don't Play Chess," *Robotics and Autonomous Systems.* Also: Brooks, "New Approaches to Robotics," *Science.*

30. A digital signal has two discrete voltage levels. An analog signal varies continuously between minimum and maximum voltages.

31. Drexler, *Engines of Creation: The Coming Era of Nanotechnology*, 78.

32. See the article about the Next Twenty Years discussion in San Francisco at: http://www.wired.com/news/technology/0,1282,37117,00.html.

33. This material is drawn from the in-depth discussion about the soul in Gresh, *Exploring Phillip Pullman's His Dark Materials: Dust, Angels, Souls, and Weird Science.*

34. Longrigg, *Greek Rational Medicine: Philosophy and Medicine from Alchaeon to the Alexandrians*, 58.

35. Cunningham, *The Anatomical Renaissance: The Resurrection of the Anatomical Projects of the Ancients*, 12.

36. Gresh, *Exploring Phillip Pullman's His Dark Materials: Dust, Angels, Souls, and Weird Science.* An entire chapter is devoted to the subject of the soul in Lois's book. In this book, we discuss the soul only as it pertains to the debate about man versus machine.

37. Originally by G. Ryle in *The Concept of Mind* (New York: Hutchinson, 1949), though the phrase "ghost in the machine" has become a common term used in many texts and articles.

38. Fogg, *Terraforming: Engineering Planetary Environments.*

39. An orbit is the time it takes for a planet or satellite to go around the sun and end up in the place from which it started. The period of Earth's orbit is usually thought to be 365 days.

40. This is the subject of one of the most entertaining *Star Trek: The Next Generation* episodes.

41. The clouds would appear at approximately 900 meters, or 3,000 feet.

42. "Evidence for a New Phase of Solid He-3," *Physical Review Letters* 28, 885 (April 1972).

43. See our book *The Science of Supervillains* for lots more on string theory.

44. See http://projects.star.t.u-tokyo.ac.jp/projects/MEDIA/xv/oc.html.

45. See http://www-cs.etsu.edu/gotterbarn/stdntppr/stats.htm concerning Jimmy Sproles and Will Byars' computer ethics course at Eastern Tennessee State University in 1998.

46. Ibid.

47. Moores, ComputerWeekly.com.

48. Ibid.

49. "Government study finds rage at boss a prime factor," The Associated Press, May 16, 2005.

50. Ibid.
51. Forno, "Security through Soundbyte: The 'Cybersecurity Intelligence' Game."
52. Leyden, "Why Is mi2g So Unpopular?"
53. Forno, "Security through Soundbyte: The 'Cybersecurity Intelligence' Game."
54. February 2001 interview conducted by Richard Thieme for *Information Security Magazine.*
55. "Cyber-Terrorism: Propaganda or Probability? Part III: How real are the risks," About.com.
56. Ibid.
57. "How 'Christianized' Do Americans Want Their Country to Be?" The Barna Group, July 26, 2004, http://www.barna.org/FlexPage.aspx?Page=BarnaUpdate&BarnaUpdateID=168.
58. Ibid.
59. Gould, Stephen J., "Evolution as Fact and Theory," *Discover,* May 1981.
60. See http://www.sciam.com/article.cfm?articleID=000D4FEC-7D5B-1D07-8E49809EC588EEDF&pageNumber=1&catID=2.
61. Rennie, "15 Answers to Creationist Nonsense."
62. See http://www.bt.com/sphere/insights/pearson/human_evolution.htm.
63. Some of this information, which was not in the movie, comes from the manga version of Nausicaa, reprinted in English by Viz Comics.
64. *Nausicaa of the Valley of the Wind* by Hayao Miyazaki, Vol. 1, VIZ LLC; February 11, 2004, 130.
65. "What Price the Environment? An Analysis of Japanese Public Awareness of Environmental Issues." Mike Danaher of Central Queensland University, Queensland, Australia. m.danaher@cqu.edu.au.
66. Orrell, David. *Gaia Theory: Science of the Living Earth,* http://www.gaianet.fsbusiness.co.uk/gaiatheory.html.
67. Lovelock, *Healing Gaia.*
68. Lovelock, *Gaia: A New Look at Life on Earth.*
69. Orrell, *Gaia Theory: Science of the Living Earth.*
70. From J. E. Lovelock's lecture "The Evolving Gaia Theory," presented at the United Nations University on September 25, 1992, in Tokyo.
71. Ibid.
72. Orrell, *Gaia Theory: Science of the Living Earth.*
73. Ibid.

74. This material is drawn from the in-depth discussion about parallel worlds in Gresh, *Exploring Phillip Pullman's His Dark Materials: Dust, Angels, Souls, and Weird Science.*

75. See http://www.bbc.co.uk/science/horizon/2001/paralleluni.shtml.

76. Tegmark, www.sciam.com.

77. Ibid.

78. Ibid.

79. de Grasse Tyson and Goldsmith, *Origins: Fourteen Billion Years of Cosmic Evolution,* 99.

80. Kaku, *Parallel Worlds,* 5. Kaku is the Henry Semat Professor of Theoretical Physics at the Graduate Center of the City University of New York. He's the author of many famous books and articles about hyperspace and parallel worlds.

81. Ibid.

82. Ibid.

83. http://www.nationmaster.com/encyclopedia/Copenhagen-interpretation.

84. Appenzeller, "Someplace Like Earth," 68.

85. Kaku, *Parallel Worlds,* 5

86. http://www.dictionary.net/virtual+reality.

87. Millard, "Whatever Happened to Virtual Reality?"

88. Ibid., interview with Rob Enderle

89. Hormann, Jeffrey S., "Virtual Reality: The Future of Law Enforcement Training," http://www.totse.com/en/law/justice_for_all/vrlawen.html.

90. Ibid.

91. McCloy, Rory and Robert Stone, "Science, Medicine, and the Future: Virtual Reality in Surgery," http://bmj.bmjjournals.com/cgi/content/full/323/7318/912.

92. Ibid.

93. Ibid.

94. "Virtual Reality Games May Help Stroke Victims Regain Mobility," http://www.nbc5.com/health/4483213/detail.html, May 12, 2005.

95. Ibid.

96. McCloy, Rory and Robert Stone, "Science, Medicine, and the Future: Virtual Reality in Surgery," http://bmj.bmjjournals.com/cgi/content/full/323/7318/912.

97. Hormann, "Virtual Reality: The Future of Law Enforcement Training."

98. Ibid.

99   Ibid.

100 Ibid.

101 Pescovitz, David, "Touching the Future of Virtual Reality,"
http://www.coe.berkeley.edu/labnotes/0903/mcmains.html, September
2003.

102 Ibid.

103 Ibid.

104 Acronym for computer-aided design. A CAD system is a combination of
hardware and software that enables engineers and architects to design
everything from furniture to airplanes. In addition to the software, CAD
systems require a high-quality graphics monitor; a mouse, light pen, or
digitizing tablet for drawing; and a special printer or plotter for printing
design specifications.

105 Pescovitz, "Touching the Future of Virtual Reality."

Bibliography

1. The Origins of Anime

1. The Anime Powerhouse.
   http://www.tapanime.com/Subpages/theinfo.html.
2. Patten, Fred. "A Capsule History of Anime." Animation World Network,
   http://www.awn.com/mag/issue1.5/articles/patten1.5.html.
3. O'Connell, Michael. "A Brief History of Anime." Animedia100.com,
   http://www.animedia100.com/news&features/a_briefhistory.htm.
4. McCarthy, Helen. *Anime! A Beginner's Guide to Japanese Animation.*
   London: Titan Books, 1993.
5. Schodt, Frederick. *Manga! Manga! The World of Japanese Comics.* New
   York: Kodansha International, 1983.
6. "Welcome to Anime Adrenaline,"
   http://www.animeadrenaline.com/manga.shtmol
7. Albanese, Giuseppe. "Anime Check-List," www.animechecklist.net.
8. Lambiek Comiclopedia. "Osamu Tezuka."
   http://www.lambiek.net/tezuka.htm.
9. Article on "Osamu Tezuka,"
   http://www.routt.net/Gelfling/manga/tezuka.html.
10. Wilhelmina, Nina. "History of Manga and Anime," http://www.
    geocities.com/rainforestwind/wind10.htm.
11. O'Connell, Michael. "A Brief History of Anime." Otakon 1999 program
    book, http://www.corneredangel.com/amwess/papers/history.html.

2. Mecha

12. "Hot Topics: Science of James Bond," November 15, 2002, http://www.bbc.co.uk/science/hottopics/jamesbond/bondgadgets.shtml.
13. Wade, Mark, "The Military Gets Mightier" BBC News Online, January 12, 2001 http://news.bbc.co.uk/1/hi/sci/tech/1112411.stm.
14. de Bakker, Liesbeth, "The World's Most Energy Efficient Robot" July 8, 2000, Radio Netherlands, http://www.rnw.nl/science/html/robots000807.html.
15. Weiss, Peter, "Dances With Robots," Science News Online, June 30, 2001 http://www.sciencenews.org/20010630/bob8.asp.
16. Hillman, Tyler, "Professor Beings Research on Futuristic Exoskeleton," *The Daily Californian*, January 30, 2002 http://www.dailycal.org/article.asp?id=7517. 17."James Bond's Gadgets,"
18. Fairley, Miki, "'Thought-Control' Prostheses—Soon a Reality," The O&P Edge, May 2005, http://www.oandp.com/news.
19. Nighswonger, Gregg. "New Polymers and Nanotubes Add Muscle to Prosthetic Limbs." *Medical Device & Diagnostic Industry* magazine, August 1999, http://www.devicelink.com/mddi/archive/99/08/004.html.
20. Gresh, Lois H. *TechnoLife 2020: A Day in the World of Tomorrow.* Toronto: ECW Press, 2001.
21. Gresh, Lois H. and Robert Weinberg. *The Science of James Bond.* Hoboken, NJ: John Wiley & Sons, Inc., 2006.
22. Gresh, Lois H. and Robert Weinberg. *The Science of Supervillains.* Hoboken, NJ: John Wiley & Sons, Inc., 2004.
23. Lois M. Gresh and Robert Weinberg. *The Science of Superheroes.* Hoboken, NJ: John Wiley & Sons, Inc., 2002.
24. See "What is Biomimetics?" at The Centre for Bimimetics at Reading University, http://www.rdg.ac.uk/Biomim/home.htm
25. "Smart Materials," *Scientific American*, May 1996. http://www.sciam.com/explorations/050596explorations.html.
26. See "Smart Materials" at Sandia National Laboratories, http://endo.sandia.gov 26.
27. Zey, Michael G. *The Future Factor: The Five Forces Transforming Our Lives and Shaping Human Destiny.* New York: McGraw-Hill, 2000.
28. O'Malley, Chris. "The Binary Man: Step One," *Popular Science,* March 1999.
29. Lawson, Guy, "The Coach Who Will Put You in The Zone - Tech 2010," *New York Times Magazine,* June 11, 2000.

30. K. Eric Drexler, as quoted in: Gross, Michael. *Travels to the Nanoworld: Miniature Machinery in Nature and Technology.* Massachusetts: Perseus Publishing, 1999.
31. Collins, Philip, & Avouris, Phaedon, "Nanotubes for Electronics," ScientificAmerican.com, Dec 1, 2000.
32. Anderson, Mark. "Mega Steps Toward the Nanochip," *Wired* magazine, April 27, 2001, http://www.wired-vig.wired.com/news/technology/0,1282,43324,00.html.
33. Anderson, Mark. "Becoming Your Own Hospital," *Wired* magazine, November 11, 2000, http://www.wired-vig.wired.com/news/technology/0,1282,40120,00.html.
34. Swissler, Mary Ann. "Microchips to Monitor Meds," *Wired* magazine, September 28, 2000, http://www.wired-vig.wired.com/news/technology/0,1282,39070,00.html.
35. "The Robot Hall of Fame (tm) Second Annual Induction Ceremony," Monday, October 11, 2004, http://www.robothalloffame.org/.
36. Gross, Michael, *Travels to the Nanoworld: Miniature Machinery in Nature and Technology.* Massachusetts: Perseus Publishing, 1999.

3. Artificial Intelligence

37. Gresh, Lois H. and Robert Weinberg. *The Computers of Star Trek.* New York: Basic Books, 1999.
38. Brooks, Rodney. "Elephants Don't Play Chess," *Robotics and Autonomous Systems.* North Holland: Elsevier Science Publishers, 1990. Also: Brooks, Rodney. "New Approaches to Robotics," *Science,* September 3, 1991.
39. Drexler, K. Eric. *Engines of Creation: The Coming Era of Nanotechnology.* New York: Anchor Books/Doubleday, 1986.
40. Oakes, Chris, "The Year 2020 Explained," Wired News, July 5, 2000 http://www.wired.com/news/technology/0,1282,37117,00.html.
41. Gresh, Lois H. *Exploring Phillip Pullman's His Dark Materials: Dust, Angels, Souls, and Weird Science* New York: St. Martin's Press, forthcoming in 2005-2006.
42. Longrigg, James. *Greek Rational Medicine: Philosophy and Medicine from Alcmaeon to the Alexandrians.* New York: Routledge Press, 1993.
43. Cunningham, Andrew. *The Anatomical Renaissance: The Resurrection of the Anatomical Projects of the Ancients.* Aldershot, United Kingdom: Ashgate, 1997.

4. Colonies in Space

44. Fogg, Martyn J. *Terraforming: Engineering Planetary Environments.* Warrendale, PA: SAE International, 1995.
45. Stern, David P., and Mauricio Peredo. "Lagrangian Points," The Exploration of the Earth's Magnetosphere, http://wwwistp.gsfc.nasa.gov/Education/wlagran.html.
46. O'Neill, Gerard K. "The Colonization of Space," *Physics Today,* September 1974.
47. O'Neill, Gerard K. *The High Frontier.* New York: William Morrow and Co., 1977.
48. "Space Settlement," http://members.aol.com/oscarcombs/settle.htm.
49. Darling, David. "Space Colony." *The Encyclopedia of Astrobiology, Astronomy, and Spaceflight,* http://www.daviddarling.info/encyclopedia/S/spacecolony.html.
50. Baez, John. "Lagrange Points." October 23, 2004, http://math.ucr.edu/home/baez/lagrange.html.
51. "O'Neill Cylinder Encyclopedia Article," http://search.localcolorart.com/search/encyclopedia/O%27Neill_cylinder/.
52. "Bernal Sphere Encyclopedia Article," http://search.localcolorart.com/search/encyclopedia/Bernal_sphere/.
53. Profile of Tomino Yoshiyuki. *Anime Academy,* http://www.animeacademy.com/profile_tomino_yoshiyuki.php.
54. "The One Year War," *Gundam Colony,* http://members.fortunecity.com/heero195/1yearwar.html.
55. "Space Colony (Gundam)," http://en.wikipedia.org/wiki/Space_Colony_(Gundam).
56. Stern, Dr. David P. "The L4 and L5 Lagrangian Points." NASA Web site, September 24, 2004, http://www.spof.gsfc.nasa.gov/stargaze/Slagrng2.htm.

5. Policing an Anime Future

57. Treder, Mike. "Molecular Nanotechnology Fully Loaded with Benefits and Risks." *Small Times,* January 5, 2004, http://www.smalltimes.com/document_display.cfm?document_id=7161.

58.   Rex, Chiroptera. "Ghost in the Shell: Stand Alone Complex Review."
      TV.com, http://www.tv.com/users/Chiroptera_Rex/profile.php.
59.   "Ghost in the Shell Encyclopedia Article,"
      http://search.localcolorart.com/search/encyclopedia/Ghost_in_the_Shell/.
60.   Page, Douglas. "Marsupial Robots Populate Ground Zero," February 1,
      2002, http://firechief.com/mag/firefighting_marsupial_robots_populate/.
61.   "So What Is Project ECHELON?" Crazylinux.net, 2001,
      http://www.crazylinux.net/photos.htm.
62.   "The Paranoids Were Right!" March 9, 1998, http://www.
      chrononhotonthologos.com/lawnotes/wiretap.htm.
63.   "From Castle Walls to Firewalls: Rapid Growth in Computer Crime,"
      Banking 2000, http://www.bankingmm.com/e-Commerce/
      computer_crime.htm.
64.   Lynch, Jim. "Web crime climbs in metro area." *The Detroit News*, August
      10, 2004, http://www.detnews.com/2004/technology/0408/10/a01-
      237792.htm.
65.   Sarkar, Dibya. "DHS, DOJ Plan Cybercrime Survey." FCW.com, January
      13, 2005, http://www.fcw.com/fcw/articles/2005/0110/web-survey-01-13-
      05.asp.
66.   Moores, Simon. "Thought for the Day: Cyberterrorism or Cyberhype?"
      ComputerWeekly.com, April 15, 2004,
      http://www.computerweekly.com/Article129905.htm.
67.   Sproles, Jimmy, and Will Byars. "Statistics on Cyber-terrorism." Eastern
      Tennessee State University, 1998, http://www-cs.etsu.edu/gotterbarn/
      stdntppr/stats.htm.
68.   Berinato, Scott. "The Truth about Cyberterrorism." *CIO* magazine, March
      15, 2002, http://www.cio.com/archive/031502/truth.html.
69.   "Cyber-Terrorism: Propaganda or Probability?" About.com,
      http://antivirus.about.com/library/weekly/aa090502c.htm.
70.   Leyden, John. "Why is mi2g so unpopular?" *The Register*, November 21,
      2002, http://www.theregister.co.uk/2002/11/21/why_is_mi2g_so_
      unpopular/.
71.   Forno, Richard. "Security through Soundbyte: The Cybersecurity Intelli-
      gence Game." *The Age*, November 22, 2002,
      http://www.theage.com.au/articles/2002/11/22/1037697858074.html?
      oneclick=true.

6. Anime Evolves

72. "Psychokinesis Encyclopedia Article,"
http://search.localcolorart.com/search/encyclopedia/Psychokinesis/.

73. Williams, Fred. "The Evolution Definition Shell Game." October
2000, http://www.evolutionfairytale.com/articles_debates/
evolutiondefinition.htm.

74. Bowler, Peter J. "History of Darwinism." BBC Evolution Web site,
http://www.bbc.co.uk/education/darwin/leghist/bowler.htm.

75. Rose, Steven. "Darwin, Genes and Determinism." BBC Evolution Web
site, http://www.bbc.co.uk/education/darwin/leghist/rose.htm.

76. Dawkins, Richard. "Darwin and Darwinism." BBC Evolution Web site,
http://www.bbc.co.uk/education/darwin/leghist/dawkins.htm.

77. Jackson, Rev. Michael. "A Christian Response to Darwinian Theories of
Evolution." BBC Evolution Web site,
http://www.bbc.co.uk/education/darwin/leghist/jackson.htm.

78. Moran, Laurence. "Evolution Is a Fact and a Theory." The Talk.Origins
Archive, http://www.talkorigins.org/faqs/evolution-fact.html.

79. Boyle, Alan. "Human Evolution at the Crossroads." MSNBC.com,
http://msnbc.msn.com/id/7103668/page/3/.

80. Elders, Wilfred. "Problems with 'Flood' Geology,"
http://www.chem.tufts.edu/science/FrankSteiger/elders-flood-report.htm.

81. "Creation and Evolution in Public Education." Infomedia, Inc., 2004,
http://encyclopedia.lockergnome.com/s/b/Creation_and_evolution_in_pu
blic_education#Early_law.

82. Rennie, John. "15 Answers to Creationist Nonsense." *Scientific American*,
July 2002, http://www.sciam.com/article.cfm?articleID=000D4FEC-
7D5B-1D07-8E49809EC588EEDF&pageNumber=1&catID=2.

83. Palme, Jacob. "The Future of Homo Sapiens; the Future of Human Evolution." December 7, 2004. http://web4health.info/en/aux/homo-
sapiens-future.html

84. Pearson, Ian. "The Future of Human Evolution." Sphere,
http://www.bt.com/sphere/insights/pearson/human_evolution.htm.

85. Diamond, Jared. *The Third Chimpanzee: The Evolution and Future of the
Human Animal.* New York: HarperCollins, 1992.

86. Garreau, Joel. *Radical Evolution.* New York: Doubleday, 2005.

87. Abraham, Ralph. *Chaos, Gaia, Eros.* New York: HarperCollins, 1994.

88. Bunyard, Peter, ed. *Gaia in Action: Science of the Living Earth.* Edinburgh: Floris Books, 1996.
89. Lovelock, James. *Gaia: A New Look at Life on Earth.* Oxford: Oxford University Press, 1979.
90. Lovelock, James. *Healing Gaia.* New York: Harmony Books, 1991.
91. Maturana, Humberto R. and Francisco J. Varela. *The Tree of Knowledge.* Boston: Shambala, 1987.

7. Parallel Universes

92. Gresh, Lois H. *Exploring Phillip Pullman's His Dark Materials: Dust, Angels, Souls, and Weird Science* New York: St. Martin's Press, forthcoming in 2005/2006.
93. Tegmark, Max. "Parallel Universes." 2003, p. 41 www.sciam.com.
94. deGrasse Tyson, Neil, and Donald Goldsmith. *Origins: Fourteen Billion Years of Cosmic Evolution.* New York: W.W. Norton & Co., 2004.
95. Kaku, Michio. *Parallel Worlds.* New York: Doubleday, 2005.
96. See "The Copenhagen Interpretation of Quantum Mechanics," at http://www.nationmaster.com/encyclopedia/Copenhagen-interpretation.
97. Appenzeller, Tim. "Someplace Like Earth." *National Geographic,* December 2004.

8. The Future of Virtual Reality

98. Hall, Justin. "Signs of .hack." Chanpon, Multi Cultural Japan Online, December 29, 2004, http://www.chanpon.org/archive/2004/12/29/20h01m32s.
99. "Serial Experiments Lain Review." *Animetique,* http://animetique.com/animeview.asp?ID=24.
100. "Dot Hackers." http://www.blackwings.net/hack/index.php
101. Bartle, Richard. "The Future of Virtual Reality." January 21, 1999, http://www.mud.co.uk/richard/vrfuture.htm.
102. Heiss, Janice J. "The Future of Virtual Reality: Part Two of a Conversation with Jaron Lanier." Sun Developer Network, February 25, 2003, http://java.sun.com/features/2003/02/lanier_qa2.html.

103. "Virtual Reality." Dictionary.net Jargon File, June 29, 2001, http://www.dictionary.net/virtual+reality.
104. Millard, Elizabeth. "Whatever Happened to Virtual Reality?" *NewsFactor Technology News*, August 30, 2002, http://www.newsfactor.com/perl/story/19242.html.

Acknowledgments

T he authors would like to thank Matthew Weinberg and Daniel Gresh, without whose help this book would never have been written. Nor would it have been as complete. As usual, we'd also like to thank our agent, Lori Perkins, for selling this book and for having confidence in it and in us long after the patience of a saint would have run out.

Musically, Bob would like to thank the anime *Beck* for "Hit in America," and Lois would like to thank the anime *Metropolis* for "I Can't Stop Loving You."